D1267090

NEVER AGAIN!

NEVER AGAIN!
A Program for Survival

MEIR KAHANE

Nash Publishing
Los Angeles

Copyright © 1971 by Meir Kahane

All rights reserved. No part of this book
may be reproduced in any form or by any means
without permission in writing from the publisher.

Library of Congress Catalog Card Number: 73-167530
Standard Book Number: 8402-1239-9

Published simultaneously in the United States and Canada
by Nash Publishing Corporation, 9255 Sunset Boulevard,
Los Angeles, California 90069.

Printed in the United States of America

First printing

DEDICATION

There was never the slightest question in my mind as to whom this book would be dedicated. It stands as my grateful thanks to the real heroes of the Jewish resistance of our times. We, the generation of the Holocaust, that stupefying tragedy that was the climax to centuries of beatings, pogroms, and degradation, have witnessed a revival of Jewish pride and self-respect. We behold an awakening of Jewish Identity. Above all, we

see a different Jew arising from the ashes and decay of
Auschwitz. It is a Jew who pauses to look the world
in the eye; to stare directly at those who, for centuries,
burned and stabbed and drowned and hanged and
gassed us; to softly say: Up against the wall, world.

With the bitter memories of the shtetl disappearing
in the flames of the crematoria and the tear-stained
pages of Jewish history, Jews have grown sick unto
death of suffering and martyrdom, weary of endless
mourner's prayers and kaddish. They are Jews who
have dropped the Christian concepts inherited in the
Exile and who no longer turn the other cheek. They are
Jews whose enemies have taught them their lessons
well. They are Jews who prefer peace but who will
now fight and win.

To the members of the Jewish Defense League, who
raised the banner of Jewish pride and strength in the
Exile, this book is dedicated. They are the real heroes
of the new Jewish phenomenon. They marched while
others deplored; they fought back while others cowered;
they climbed the barricades for Soviet Jews while others
condemned; they put into practice the words of this
book. Some day, when the events of our time are written in the pages of history, the truth will be known and
their names will be inscribed for all time as one more
link in the glorious chain of Jewish courage and resistance. The Jewish people owe them a great debt.

I would also like to add my heartfelt thanks to Ber-
tram Zweibon, the co-founder of the Jewish Defense

League, without whose help neither the organization nor this book would exist.

Finally, my gratitude and love to my beloved wife and children who have endured more than any others in my absence from home. I would not be worthy of their love or respect had I done otherwise, and all that I have done has been for them.

CONTENTS

NEVER AGAIN!

NEVER AGAIN!

We have seen the mounds of corpses and visited the camps where they killed us. We have stood in the now empty rooms where once Jews were driven to stand in their nakedness and breathe their last. We stood alone and not alone. By our side were the ghosts of those who were no longer, whose blood was shed like water because Jewish blood is considered cheap. We saw their outstretched hands and looked into their burning and soul-searing eyes that peered into our very being and heard them say:

Never again. Promise us. Never again.

In fulfillment of that promise this book was written. *Never again.*

THE DEAFENING SILENCE

On May 13, 1939, a ship sailed out of the German city of Hamburg. On board were 930 Jews sailing from their native land, leaving behind all that they owned, turning their backs on a lifetime and a Fatherland gladly. It was the worst of times in the Third Reich as the madness of Adolph Hitler gained irrational momentum. Six years of Nazi rule had escalated into terror, concentration camps, beatings, and degradation, and nine hundred and thirty Jews were leaving the nightmare that had once been their home. They were among the last Jews who were given the opportunity to leave the land of the Aryans alive before the night of the Panzers descended upon Europe.

In all this world, of all the many ports, of all the nations that existed, only one decided to grant refuge to 930 desperate refugees. In their pockets, the German

Jews held entry visas to Cuba and in their hearts grateful thanks to the Havana government that, alone of all the countries in the world, had agreed to accept them. But Jews are, usually, too hasty in their gratitude to the nations of the world, and before they even reached Havana they were informed that the Cuban government would not allow them to enter. The visas, it was ruled, were illegal.

The ship reached Havana and docked, a figurative stone's throw from Miami Beach where other Jews played in the surf and watched the dogs race in the evenings; in the very backyard of Collins Avenue where other Jews tanned themselves and ate from the legendary Jewish menus and enjoyed the good life. How close to the American Nirvana stood the 930 and how far from salvation they really were.

The drama unfolded as millions of Americans watched. Cuba remained adamant. Under a wave of anti-Semitism that appeared in Cuban newspapers and among its politicians, Havana insisted that the visas were illegal, that she had already taken in Jews, and—the unkindest cut of them all—what about the great colossus of democracy to the north, the United States?

The question was a good one and grew more cogent as it became clear that neither Cuba nor any other country was prepared to accept the unwelcome refugees. It became pressing as the days passed and the German ship lifted anchor, setting sail for the grim mockery that was called home. Home to Hitler went the 930.

And the American Jewish brothers and sisters?

What were they doing? What awesome rallies and demonstrations were being organized? What militant and angry Jewish groups were mounting protests to show the world that Jews would not sit idly by while almost a thousand of their flesh and blood were being dragged back to hell?

Surely those organizations and leaders, who in years to come would surge forward on behalf of the civil rights movement—even to the point of willingly breaking the law—when the problem was not exactly death camps but the right of people to sit in the front of a bus in Birmingham or to drink soda at the same fountain as whites in Jackson—surely such zealots for human freedom and rights would climb the barricades on behalf of their fellow Jews who faced the specter of death? Surely all the liberals and humanists, who in the future would go to Selma confident that they would overcome if only they made the necessary sacrifices, were prepared to make at least those same sacrifices on behalf of their own people in this year of Hitler.

The silence is deafening. The record is obscenely empty of any vigorous sacrifice on the part of those Jewish leaders who are supposed to lead us and those Jewish groups organized to defend us. Those who went to jail in Selma for the cause of civil rights did not even consider the possibility of chaining themselves to the White House gates to call attention to the plight of the 930 who, themselves, symbolized millions of others on the brink of slaughter.

Aside from efforts by the Joint Distribution Committee—which was not a membership organization and which was created solely to aid refugees—the Jewish Establishment groups limited their efforts to respectable, pious petitions to Franklin Delano Roosevelt.

Franklin Delano Roosevelt. For American Jewry there was the Almighty, and there was Roosevelt—and not necessarily in that order. Roosevelt, for whom all Jews voted. Roosevelt, upon whose passing all Jews wept as if for a close, beloved relative. Roosevelt, for whom they will not speedily build monuments in Israel.

Franklin Roosevelt watched as 930 Jews sailed along the Atlantic coast on their way back to Hitler. He could have opened the doors and he did not. He could have saved not only nine hundred but nine thousand and nine hundred thousand. But he and all the Western democracies at whose altars Jews worshipped with such piety, did not lift a finger for the Jew. The political theory of relativity was clear: When the world is in trouble it is demanded of the Jew that he help, because he is a human. When the Jew is oppressed, humanity is freed from any obligation because it is a Jewish problem.

Roosevelt heard the pleas of Jewish leaders and sadly told them that he could do nothing. There was, after all, a quota system in effect, and the German quota was filled. If so, cried Jews, mortgage the quota to future years. Let the 930 come in, and let their numbers be counted to next year's quota or the next decade's. Surely some way could be thought up by a brilliant President for whom we voted.

But the President of the United States could not do

such things. Bending the law was a thing that one did not do; Roosevelt never bent the law. And so he sympathized but could do nothing. With deep regrets he went home.

And so, as the *St. Louis* came close enough to Miami for the refugees to see the lights of the city where, at that moment, Jews were laughing and amusing themselves; as the *St. Louis* mournfully headed past the American shore followed by United States Coast Guard ships under orders to prevent any refugee from jumping overboard; as the President of the United States sympathetically refused to save 930 Jews and went home, the American Jewish Establishment slipped silently into the night and went home too.

There were no loud and angry protests. There was no violation of the law. There were none of the things that certain Jewish leaders later did for civil rights in Selma and Jackson. Like thieves in the night we slunk away and went home.

And as American Jews went home, so did the 930. Look homeward, 930 future angels. Look homeward to Hitler. Behind them they left a grief-stricken, if paralyzed, liberal and Jewish community. For let it not be said that American Jews did not feel for their brothers and sisters. *The New York Times,* in one of its impeccable editorials, might have spoken for all the Jewish leaders, organizations, and masses when it wrote:

"We can only hope that some hearts will soften somewhere and some refuge be found. The cruise of the *St. Louis* cries to high heaven of man's inhumanity to man."

Indeed. And the editorial of *The New York Times* stank of the fraud of the respectable people whose sole contribution to the cries of the refugees was a "hope that some hearts would soften somewhere." Never was there a thought, either in the minds of *The Times* or the Jewish Establishment that, perhaps, actions to help the softening process might be attempted. Never did the Respectables consider taking to the streets to demand justice for their 930 brothers and sisters. Sympathy yes, militancy never. And so the 930 passed into history. Their immediate end was produced by the Germans, but no Jew who sat by silently can really sleep well nights.

And then came the darkness. With a terrible suddenness, the war that all pacifists and mothers and isolationists sought to avoid came anyhow. Those who had cheered Munich for bringing them peace in their time suddenly understood what a minority of "warmongers" had seen all along, that one could not avoid being eaten by the alligator merely by feeding one's neighbor to him. Munich had only guaranteed a holocaust and placed the Free World at a bitter disadvantage.

World War II came with its lightening blitzkriegs and its Panzer divisions knifing through Poland as if it were soft butter. It came with its Luftwaffe bombing and strafing a paper tiger called France, whose Maginot Line proved to be as decadent as those who built it and believed in it.

And, now, we Jews understood also. Now we understood that the few who had warned us that the man named Hitler really meant it and that the holocaust was indeed coming, were not quite as paranoid as our leaders had told us. Suddenly it was clear that those who had gone through Polish and Lithuanian and German and Czech and Hungarian towns and cities crying, "Jews, get out! A fire is burning!" were not as foolish or as mad as our experts had told us. Suddenly the Jewish community of Eastern Europe faced extermination.

The mind was unable to cope with the thought. Extermination—in this, the twentieth century! Extermination—in this era of liberalism, secularism, and science! The impossible had come about, and as great as was the destruction of human beings was the destruction of liberal illusions. All that could not possibly have happened began to happen. All that could not conceivably have occurred, came about.

From every part of Europe the Jew was gathered up in a nightmarish parody of his prayers. From the four corners of the continent he was collected—not for redemption, but for extermination. That which began as rumors—not to be believed—soon became an incontrovertible fact. They were killing Jews in Europe; they were destroying them by the millions. They were gassing them, they were burning them, they were exterminating our brothers and sisters. By late 1942 and early 1943 we knew. Two years before the war came to an end, Jewish organizations knew. Jewish leaders, throughout the world, knew. Jewish organizations in the United States knew that a holocaust was raging and that the destroyer had been given leave to destroy. Let no leaders or groups protest their ignorance. There are, in the end, only two groups who continue to maintain that they know nothing of the death camps then. The Germans there and some Jewish leaders here. They are both liars.

We knew that they were taking whole towns to death camps. We knew that they were decimating entire areas. We knew that they showed no mercy to women or children and that, to Nazis, the Biblical injunction was to be strictly followed: "One law shall there be for all of you." We knew the names: Dachau, Buchenwald, Treblinka, Bergen-Belsen—and Auschwitz.

Auschwitz. Where every day twelve thousand Jews were gassed to death as the Germans reached the zenith of efficiency in the art of "Zyklon B." Twelve thousand people every day. As American Jews celebrated their weddings—there were twelve thousand less Jews on this earth. As they reveled in their expensive Bar Mitzvahs—there were twelve thousand fewer of their co-religionists. As they spent a pleasant Sunday at home—twelve thousand brothers and sisters alleviated the population explosion. And all this we knew. As early as 1942 we knew, and as early as 1943 we had been informed about the horror of Auschwitz.

And how they cried out to us: Letters and pleas from inside the Hitlerian holocaust poured into the free Jewish world, with none as poignant as the bitter, pleading messages sent by the saintly Rabbi Michael Dov Ben Weissmandel of Slovakia. Rabbi Weissmandell, the fervently Orthodox rabbi who lived through the Auschwitz era and who single-handedly saved Jews from under the eyes of the Nazis. Rabbi Weissmandel, who himself was captured and placed on a transport train to Auschwitz, and who wrote to Jewish leaders in Turkey, Switzerland, and the United States to shake the world on behalf of their brethren. There was no time, he screamed. Do whatever has to be done. In agony he wrote:

"Drop all other business to get this done. Remember that one day of your idleness kills 12,000 souls . . .

"How is it that all our pleadings affect you less than the whimperings of a beggar standing in your doorway?

"We have told you the truth many times. Is it possible that you believe our murderers more than you believe us?

"May G-d open your eyes and give you heart to rescue in these last hours, the remainder . . ."

Rabbi Weissmandel never received a reply to this letter. But then, why should *he* have been better than those who died in the death camps? They too cried out, and there was no answer; and American Jewish leadership can never say: Our hands have not had a hand in the shedding of that blood . . . .

So many could have been saved! Jews were transported to Auschwitz by railroad; and the cattle cars, jammed with pitiful candidates for death, rolled daily down the rail lines into Auschwitz. Bomb the rail lines! came the cry from Europe. Bomb the bridges over which the lines run. Bomb the death camp areas so that the massive installations will be put out of commission. The Czech underground had furnished the free world with maps of the lines and the general area. All that remained to be done was for Allied bombers to drop their bombs and to do to Auschwitz what they were doing daily to other targets throughout Europe.

Alas, it could be done. In a letter to Chaim Weizmann, president of the World Zionist Organization, the British Foreign Ministry stated that the matter had received "the most careful consideration" but could not be implemented "in view of the very great technical difficulties involved."

And in the United States the charade was repeated. As Jewish leaders asked Franklin Roosevelt (still President; still the darling of Jewish voters) to save their brethren, he nodded sympathetically but allowed as it was impossible because of "the technical difficulties."

Technical difficulties. The man whose bombers roamed the earth, blasting everything that moved. The man whose B-17s had penetrated Ploesti in Rumania could not overcome the "technical difficulties" involved in bombing the Auschwitz area.

Let it be. It is not our purpose to condemn Roosevelt. Those who still have trust in the Roosevelts or the Churchills or the Vaticans of the world are fools, learning nothing from history and dooming us all to repeat the holocausts therein. It is not the Roosevelts who are the villains of the Holocaust.

What did *we* do? That is the question, the question that gives us no peace and allows no respite for our seared souls. When Franklin Roosevelt dismissed his Jewish voters, what did they do? What did the leaders of the prestigious organizations, whose reason for being was to defend Jews, do in this most awesome of times?

When told that Jews would have to die, what was their reaction?

I know Jewish leaders who went to Mississippi as Freedom Riders because their hearts ached for their fellow human beings, and that was good. I know Jewish leaders who went to Jackson and broke the law and defied the government because they felt the pain of the oppressed in the South. I know rabbis who went to Selma and to jail for the right of blacks to equal opportunities in employment, in education, and at the polls. I know Jews who endure suffering and imprisonment for Blacks and Puerto Ricans and Chicanos and Indians at home and risk bloody heads and broken arms at demonstrations for Vietnamese, Laotians, Cambodians, Greeks, and South African Zulus abroad. I know Jewish youth who confront their parents with bitter signs that read; Your Silence Is Killing Me—and they refer to everything but the Jewish issue. I know Jews who cannot sleep because of their concern for humanity and who give of their days and nights for their fellow human beings, but Jewish suffering leaves them strangely apathetic.

I know of no Jewish leaders whose bodies so ached with the pain of their slaughtered brothers that they decided to break the law to shake the world from its apathy. I know of no Jewish leaders who decided that a world that did not care about the suffering of the Jew could not be allowed the respite of an innocent conscience or who decided that it was the Jewish obligation to allow the world neither slumber nor peace until Jewish lives had been saved. I know of no leaders who decided that, when all else failed, the threat of Jewish extermination made it a moral imperative to do whatever was necessary and who then chained themselves to the White House gates and went to jail so that the problem would be aired. I know of no rabbis who were driven by the Biblical injunction, "Thou shalt not stand idly by thy brother's blood," to call their flock into the streets and to sit there in cold anger at the refusal of the United States to save lives.

Consider what would have happened had Jewish leaders of every major organization, together with rabbis from all over the country, called for mass sit-downs of hundreds of thousands of Jews in the streets of Washington, New York, Chicago, and other major cities. Picture the streets filled with Jews of all kinds: men, women, children, employers, workers, religious and nonobservant, people of the Right and those of the Left, sitting and chanting their agony and their anger. Imagine all of them led by the prestigious and respectable leaders and rabbis demanding: Bomb the rail lines and save our brothers or we shall not move!

Surely, the bombers would have been sent out; without a doubt the railroads would have been blasted and the cattle cars with their pitiful cargoes stopped. Line after line of Jews would have been saved, their numbers reaching into the hundreds of thousands, if not more. All of this might have been, had we fulfilled our obligations as Jews, had we been the kind of people we claim to be, had the Jewish flock not been led by leaders who crawled when they should have walked and strolled when they should have run.

Of what do we speak here? We speak of Ahavat Yisroel—the love of one Jew for another—and an absence of that love. We speak here of that which has always been the Foundation of Foundations of the Jewish people and which was not to be found when Jews needed it most.

Ahavat Yisroel—Love of Jewry. The Jewish people —wherever they may be; each Jewish individual— wherever he is, whatever his belief, whatever his place of residence, whatever the color of his skin, whatever language he temporarily speaks—*All* Jews are part of the great body, Israel. All are brothers, all are sisters, and the love of a brother to a brother and to a sister is the love of one Jew to another.

The pain of a Jew, wherever he may be, is our pain. The joy of a Jew, wherever he may be, is our joy. We are committed to going to the aid of a Jew who is in need, without distinction, without asking what kind of Jew he is. As the great Hassidic teachers would never tire of emphasizing the oneness and equality of all Jews, so must we embrace, with deepest love, all Jews, and pledge, at all times, to come to their aid.

But we did not come and we did not do that which we should and could have done.

The question, the terrible, awesome question that must clutch at our hearts and grapple with our minds and give us no peace, is: *Why?*

Why were we so silent? Why did we not do for our

own what we did for others in years to come? How could we have failed to mount the most massive of protests and how could we have refrained from climbing the barricades? Where was a Jewish leader to call for monstrous acts of civil disobedience on behalf of those awaiting monstrous gassing, shooting, burning, soaping, and degradation? Where was the Jewish leader to stand before the five million American Jews and remind them of the words of the rabbis:

"At a time when Jews are wrapped in sorrow and one of them removed himself from the community, two servant angels come and place their hands on his head, saying:

" 'This individual who removed himself from the community will not merit seeing the comfort of the community.'

"And we further learned: At a time when a community is wrapped in sorrow let no man say: 'I shall go home and eat and drink and I will be at peace with myself . . .' " (Tannit 11)

No one can say that the American Jew did not care. Jews do care. No one can say that Jewish leaders simply did not feel Jewish pain. That is not true and it is not the reason for Jewish silence. Nevertheless, millions in Europe went to their gas chambers and crematoria, and we knew of it. We knew of it and were worse than silent, for he who knows of horror and limits himself to tepid, useless, respectable, occasional efforts is worse than the one who knows and does nothing. The latter knows his sin of omission, and there is yet hope that his conscience will impel him to meaningful action. The former, however, persuades himself that he has indeed done something and is at peace with himself.

They died and we did not do what we could have done to save them. Why?

There are those who will be upset. Why raise such a painful subject? That which was done is done and buried, and what can be gained by going back over this most terrible of Jewish historical periods?

We must. We must resurrect the question because we can never resurrect those who died because of it. We must seek an answer to what happened lest it happen again, and that must never again be. We must ask why our Jewish leadership failed to act, because that same leadership still shepherds us and still speaks in our name and gives us guidance. We must learn from history so as not to repeat it. Worse, we must learn from the past because we may *be* repeating it again, this time in the case of Soviet Jewry.

In 1917, the Bolshevik revolution came to Russia and the curtain came down on one of the great sagas of Jewish history. The Russian Jew would never be the same again. The Russian Jewish community, warm and throbbing, the cream of world Jewry, was irrevocably changed.

The land that brought forth such fertile Jewish minds as Rabbi Elijah of Vilna and Rabbi Yitzhak Elchanan; the land in which sprang up the Torah centers of Volozhin and Slobodka; the country where the spirit of Zionism flowed to give life to the bones of Herzl's dream

and which saw such burning Jewish leaders as Jabotinsky, Usishkin, and Pinsker; the land of the so very warm
and beautiful Jewish masses who were oppressed by
poverty but uplifted by their faith, who dreamed their
Jewish dreams, lived their Jewish lives, and died in a
Jewish embrace; the Russia of the cheder (school) and
the pripichek (fireplace) where young little Jews learned
their Aleph Bet in preparation for taking upon their little
backs the yoke of the Kingdom of Heaven; the place
where Jews in their poverty never turned away a Jew
who was poorer than they and whose prayers were so
poignant as to reach as high as the Throne of Glory and
pierce the curtain of iron that separated the Almighty
from His suffering children. This was the Russia that was
irrevocably destroyed in 1917. In its place there arose
the Kingdom of Marx and the Fiefdom of Lenin. Communism had come to Russia and all Jews would soon
understand its full impact.

From the beginning it was clear that Judaism, as all
other religions, would be hunted down and eradicated.
Communism was a jealous mistress and could tolerate no
rivals for the love and the soul of the one she desired to
master. And so, with a zeal that would have done justice
to the Church, the high and the low priests of the new
faith searched out Judaism. Their finest tool proved to be
the Yevesekzia—the Jewish wing of the Communist
Party. It is not a new thing. There is no greater anti-
Semite than the Jewish one, and none hates the Jewish
people more than the Jewish traitor and apostate. No
traditional Jew ever searched for leaven on the eve of

Passover as the Communists sought out the tools of Judaism.

Rabbis and teachers were arrested and sent to Siberia. The schools were closed and synagogues shut down to be converted to youth clubs. No religious books were permitted to be printed, and the great works of the Bible, the Talmud, and the Jewish commentaries were banned from the Russian presses. Those who had prayer books watched over them as over precious stones, and, in the absence of religious calendars, Jews had to find some other means of learning when their holidays occurred.

With no religious schools and with private teaching of Judaism forbidden by law, the greatness that had been Russian Judaism began to wither and die. The rabbis grew grey and the elders, older still. State schools mocked and scorned Judaism, and Jewish history was distorted. Moral wedges were driven between parents and children, and religious tradition and practice were cruelly derided and hunted down.

The holidays were attacked as tools of bourgoise nationalism, intended to instill a separatist spirit into the Jew. They were condemned as hindering production plans and violating work discipline since the Jew did not labor on those days. The Passover was singled out for special assault since it oriented Jews to thinking of their nationalism and of next year in Jerusalem.

Circumcision, central to Judaism, was attacked as a barbaric rite and the Bar Mitzvah as an attempt to spiritually disfigure the young boy. Those who attended synagogue were barred from any meaningful advance in

Soviet society and were subjected to harassment and taunts.

Jewish parents watched with broken hearts and crushed spirits as their children were torn from the bosom of their people and sacrificed to strange gods in mute fulfillment of the awesome Biblical warning:

"Thy sons and thy daughters shall be given unto another people and thine eyes shall look and fail with longing for them all the day long; and there shall be no might in thine hand." (Deuteronomy 28:32)

No more poignant description of the Soviet Jewish agony can be found than the one given by Shlomo Ben Yisroel, a Yiddish journalist who visited the Soviet Union some years ago and who wrote of what he saw one Sabbath in a Russian city:

"But many of the older Jews cling to their faith with a strength that surpasses all understanding. Once, in a synagogue in another Russian city, I heard a tremulous voice behind me.

" 'Reb Yid, don't turn around. Keep your eyes on your Siddur and pretend you hear nothing. I have to talk to someone.' '

"Out of the corner of my eye I saw an old man, his face covered by the prayer shawl draped over his head. Leaning against his lectern, he spoke in a voice choked with tears. He had lost his whole family—his wife, his children, his relatives, all except one son, who now had a young son of his own, named Volodenka.

"Until he was five, Volodenka had accompanied his grandfather to synagogue. When he started school his

teacher forbade the students to attend church or synagogue, but the boy was so devoted to his grandfather that
he went anyway until, one day, a classmate reported him.
The teacher punished him, humiliated him in front of
the class, and issued a stern warning. Since then, Volodenka has not dared to go to synagogue.

"The years passed. Six months ago, eight gentile boys
attacked Volodenka and beat him up, shouting, 'Zhid!
Let's kill the dirty Zhid!' Since then the boy has been
full of fears. He clings to his grandfather and begs the old
man to explain why he is Jewish and why the others hate
him for it. The old man would have liked to teach his
grandson Jewish history, Hebrew and the Bible, but the
boy's father would not permit it, afraid that if word got
out he might lose his job, or worse.

"Soon Volodenka will be 13 years old, and the grandfather is desperate.

" 'Volodenka, I said to him,' the old man wept, 'I'll
give you anything you want. Just come to shul with me.'
But Volodenka won't do it.

"The lectern behind me shook with the old man's
sobs. Suddenly he leaned forward.

" 'I beg of you, dear friend,' he whispered, 'when you
go back to the free world, don't hold your peace. Stir up
the people, turn the world upside down if you must, but
help us! Help me so that my Volodenka will remain a
Jew.' " (Russian Sketches, published by the American
Jewish Committee.)

Who shook the world? Who turned it upside down
and who shared the agony of a grandfather for his Volo-

denka? Surely not the American Jew.

And there were so many opportunities! In the decades that stretched from 1917, there were so many golden opportunities to force the Soviets to yield and to let our people go—when the Soviets needed engineers and technicians in the 1920s, when Stalin sought recognition from Roosevelt in the 1930s, and when, in desperate need of a second front, they sent their Jewish Anti-Fascist Committee here to propagandize for support in the 1940s. Does anyone recall our grasping these opportunities to demand that Moscow's wants be withheld until they paid a Soviet Jewish price?

Can anyone remember street protests for Soviet Jews in all the decades from 1917 to 1963? Let the awesome truth be known. For nearly half a century, there was not one single, solitary mass street protest for Soviet Jewry by the Jewish community of the United States.

And we knew all that was happening. We knew that it was not only the Jewish faith that was being plowed under, but the Jewish national concept too. Other peoples were oppressed within the U.S.S.R., but at least they were able to live in their own land. At least they were able to study in their national languages; at least they were able to study their individual Latvian or Ukrainian or Lithuanian cultures; at least they could delve into their own national history. The Jew was not granted even that. What every other minority was given the Jew was denied.

For Lenin had decreed that Jews were not a nationality. They had no territory in the U.S.S.R., they had no

language or a rooted peasant class. Lacking these absolute prerequisites, they failed to qualify as a separate
national entity and would have to assimilate. Thus decreed Lenin; and Stalin, his heir, underscored the judgment by calling the Jews a "nation on paper only." Forgotten was their common history and suffering. Over
looked was their common culture and common Hebrew
and Yiddish language. The Jew was not a nation, and he
would be assimilated. As a nation he did not exist, and
as a religion he would not exist. There was only one
other choice for the new Soviet Jew: Disappear.

We knew all this and watched all this and were
silent. Already our sin is greater than we can bear. If by
our silence with Hitler we allowed millions to lose their
Jewish lives, by our failure to protest against the Soviet
Union we have permitted millions to lose their Jewish
souls.

There is little doubt that if they opened the gates of
the Soviet Union tomorrow and allowed all Jews to
leave, the majority might very well stay. If so, each and
every Jew, every single Volodenka who chooses to stay
and cut his ties with his people, is on our conscience. We
created them all. By our silence for half-a-century we
gave the Soviet Union fifty years to assimilate, integrate,
amalgamate, and dissolve these Jews.

American Jewish leaders in the past would tell the
community that they were conducting all manner of secret negotiations. Perhaps this was true; but they lacked
the sense of urgency needed to succeed, and they were
conducted with the kind of respectability that is doomed

to fail. Messages to the State Department and infrequent visits to the White House were the weapons of the Jewish Establishment. From the outset they were tepid and grotesque failures that had no chance of success and whose obvious impotence brought forth no other, more desperate, reaction by these leaders.

Indeed, when rebel-types and young people demanded that more be done, they were silenced with the eternal warning: You will only make things worse. And in the end, whatever protests first began and whatever street demonstrations were first started were the products, not of the Jewish Establishment, but of young Jews and mavericks who broke with the policy of silence. They were immediately condemned by the major Jewish organizations before they proved that their way was the only one to shake a world on behalf of Volodenka.

Today, the danger to Soviet Jewry grows with every passing hour. For almost a score of years we have had a golden opportunity to do the militant and outragous things needed to shake the world and the Soviets. From the death of Stalin in 1953, the U.S.S.R. was governed by men and institutions that were weak and incapable of the authoritarian measures practiced by the Georgian dictator. These were years of rare opportunities, and we let so many of them go. And who knows what tomorrow can bring?

We forget so easily, we whose world is encompassed by our own little problems which assume, for us, such awesome proportions. We forget so easily the final years of Stalin, the final nightmarish years of horror. The years

when Stalin gathered together the last of the Jewish intellectuals, writers, and poets and shot them. The years
when he threw hundreds of Jews into prisons because
they were "cosmopolitans." The insane and deadly
"Doctors Plot" in which the dictator accused Jewish
doctors of plotting to kill him and other Soviet leaders.

Those were the years when Stalin drew up lists of
hundreds of thousands of Jews to be sent to Siberian
camps for his own version of the Final Solution. They
were the years when Jews dared not travel too far from
their homes for fear that the secret police might come in
their absence and take away their families. They were the
years when Jews kept suitcases packed, filled with neces-
sities, and waited for the knock on the door.

G-d was good to Soviet Jewry, and Stalin died. But
what of tomorrow? Who, but the eternally trusting and
eternally proven-wrong lemming-pacifist can vouch for
the end of Stalinism? A time of increased Western isola-
tionism and growing indications of a Free World's
unwillingness to fight, is a time for adventurism and
brazenness. A time of lessened need of world public
opinion is a time of growing totalitarianism. And for the
Soviet Jew, there is something else. For him there is a
growing, logical probability of physical punishment and
assault.

There is a miracle today within the Soviet Union, and
we have observed it with our own eyes. Twenty-five
centuries ago the Prophet Ezekiel was shown a field filled
with dry, Jewish bones and was asked: Can these bones
live? We have seen the answer. They can and do. The

dry and sterile and dead bones of the young Soviet Jews have come to life, defying all logic and rationality in their defiance of the Kremlin.

Denied an opportunity to study their Jewish religion and heritage, they go to the Moscow synagogue to dance on Simchat Torah—the holiday of the Rejoicing with the Law. Most do not know what they sing; they only know that it is Jewish and thus beautiful. That is enough for them. Having been robbed of any chance to learn their history and their national culture, they now demand to go to the land that the Kremlin calls fascist, racist, and aggressor. Having been tyrannized and subjected to national-cultural genocide, they stand and shout to their oppressors: Up against the wall, Mother Russia!

And what does the Kremlin see as it watches tens of thousands of young Jews dance their Jewish dances and shout "Long Live Israel"? It sees Soviet citizens shouting their praise of a "fascist" state whose pilots shoot down Soviet pilots (because Jewish pilots are better than the Russians). And it cannot long stand for such a thing.

And what does the Soviet dictatorship see when a young Soviet Jew enters the Ministry of Interior's OVIR office that distributes exit visas for Israel? It sees a young Jew applying to go to Israel because he has an aunt in Haifa and cannot live without seeing her. But it knows full well that he has other aunts in Moscow, and what he really yearns for is to be free in his land, to be a Jew with his own people. And it cannot long abide this.

And is it, therefore, so improbable that the angry and

violent Russians, whose basic Jew-hatred has been held back only by weakness and need for the support of world-wide public opinion, will in some future date explode in a physical assault on Soviet Jews? Is there one whose soul is so at peace with himself that he can assure us that this is not a distinct possibility?

Indeed it is. And because it is, we have no time. We have not the luxury of time to call international conferences and fly hundreds of Jewish leaders thousands of miles at the cost of hundreds of thousands of dollars in Jewish money, merely to sit for three days and emerge with a resolution declaring solidarity with Soviet Jewry. We have no time for such nonsense and precious little future opportunities that we can fritter away on foolishness.

There is a need for feeling the pain of the Soviet Jew. There is a need for feeling the essence of Ahavat Yisroel. There is an obligation to do outrageous things, and there is a hallowed duty for Jewish leaders to do today the things they did not do in the past for Soviet Jews and the things they failed to do for the Six Million.

There is a need because there is no time, and we cannot repeat this too many times. On the contrary, it is incumbent upon us to shout it from the rooftops and to din it into the ears of all who would hear—or not hear. There is no time! Another holocaust could well approach! And we are pitifully silent, woefully inept.

So, once again we must ask this question.

Why? Why were we silent thirty years ago as Hitler's hand choked our brethren to death; why have we been so silent in all these years when the Kremlin's hand snatched Jewish souls away and why are we so pitifully timid today when a potential destruction may well face our Soviet Jewish brethren?

Why has the terrible plight of tortured Jewish prisoners within Arab lands brought forth only a deafening silence?

We must learn the answer or face a horror that will allow our own souls and consciences no peace all the days of our lives.

MORAL BANKRUPTCY OF THE JEWISH ESTABLISHMENT

But there is more. There is more to the moral paralysis of the Jew and of his failure to speak out for his needy and suffering brother and sister. It is not only from abroad that the cry of a Jew is unanswered. In the United States, too, there are ever-growing problems that beset Jews and that we and our Jewish leadership refuse to recognize, alleviate, or solve.

Consider the American Jewish problems we have allowed to fester and the domestic Jewish agony we have allowed to go unrepaired as we have led our own insulated and sheltered lives, as we have concentrated on our own limited and personal ambitions, as Jewish organizations and leaders have spent so much time and effort on so many other peoples and other causes.

In the end, of course, the Jewish agony that we would rather avoid dealing with because it is not in our own neighborhood or because it does not affect the ones we love or because we would rather avoid "making things worse" will indeed intensify, then become critical, and will—in the end—drag us all down together. The high and the mighty, the wealthy and the fortunate, those who have escaped the urban horrors and those who have raised themselves from the muck of poverty —all will go under together with the Jews they refused to help.

But this is small consolation as we consider carefully all the Jewish problems over which our American Jewish prestigious organizations have presided while spending our Jewish money and expending our Jewish energies for everyone else.

There is Jewish poverty in the United States. It is, of course, true that most Jews are "Rothschilds and international bankers," but there are some who are poor. In New York City, the third largest poverty group is that of the Jews. Tens of thousands of Jews live below the poverty standards set by government economic statisticians. In the urban inner city and so-called ghetto areas live thousands of Jewish families who, daily, fight poverty. Orthodox and Hassidic Jews with large families and small incomes eke out a living as factory workers, manual laborers, and low-paid civil servants.

Many of them cannot escape their identity any more than can Blacks or Puerto Ricans or Chicanos. The beard and the black frock make them easy prey for job discrimination, and there is no one to fight for their rights. Government small business loans are reserved for other minority groups, not them.

But who cares? Who cares enough to see to it that poor young Hassidic Jews are given the benefit of the same kind of tough legal aid when it comes to job discrimination as we have offered to others? Who cares enough to challenge the discriminatory practice of limiting business loans to others, and not Jews? Where are all the Jewish organizations who rush pell-mell to be *amicus curiae,* friends of the court, for every group and every cause. Jews also need friends in the court. . . .

Jewish groups can find lawyers for so many causes. Let a Xmas tree go up on the municipal lawn of a small Wyoming town, and a battery of Establishment lawyers will be prepared to go to court with their legal hatchets. Let the government announce that a Xmas stamp is contemplated and the Establishment will leap to the defense of secularism. For all this nonsense attorneys can be found. For the Jewish needy the lawyers have no time.

Those who continually prick our consciences and sear our souls for other oppressed peoples are noticeably silent when the oppressed chattel is a Jew. Our Jewish social-conscience leaders have chastised and criticized us, thundered at and admonished us. We have been told that we are sinners and have been called upon to do penance. Our transgressions against all the poor and the defenseless have been thrown up in our faces and our obligations to Blacks, Mexicans, Puerto Ricans, Eskimos, and Indians have been held up before us, lest we forget. Our Jewish organizations and our rabbis

never cease to thunder the Eleventh Commandment:
Give a Damn!

And this is good; one should care, one should give
a damn about the oppressed and the needy. But who will
give a damn about the Jewish poor and the Jewish disadvantaged? Who will care about the poor Jews of Williamsburg or Crown Heights or Brownsville in New
York City; the elderly and depressed of Mattapan-Dor-
chester in Boston or the Fairfax area in Los Angeles; the
forgotten poor of all the other major urban centers?

The antipoverty agencies are dominated by non-
Jews, and Jewish needs are arrogantly and blatantly disregarded. Anti-poverty funds have long since become a
huge pork barrel that other minority groups have
seized, and the Jew is prevented from sharing them in
any meaningful degree. Anti-semitism within these agencies is blatant and outrageous, with slurs and rhetoric
not the least of the problem. Militants employed by these
agencies have used physical violence against Jews within the poor neighborhoods and during elections for anti-
poverty councils.

There are thousands of Jews who live in the worst
slum areas of the country. They are poor Jews; they are
elderly Jews; they are frightened Jews. But, above all,
they are forgotten Jews.

They have been forgotten by our Jewish leaders and
Jewish organizations who are too busy bleeding for
others and castigating us for not caring about those
others. Their plight is seldom thought about by their
brethren in the split levels of America and no symphony

conductor or composer gives cocktail parties for them.

One can find them if he bothers to look in some of the same low income public housing projects that blacks inhabit. They sit in the prisons that pass for apartments —old and frail and terrified. They wait to die.

They are on welfare (*et tu*, Jew?) and they venture out only infrequently to buy food. The trip to the store is not the simple thing it is for the resident of more fortunate neighborhoods. Will the elderly Jew manage to return safely, with all limbs intact? It is not an academic question for the denizens of the urban jungle. And so they buy things like Matzohs and powdered milk —things that keep—so that the trips to the store may be as infrequent as possible. Most synagogues are closed or services are infrequent, for to go beyond the closed, locked, barred, and bolted door is to risk too much.

And so these elderly and poverty-stricken Jews live out their desperate lives in misery and fear. They are the only Jews left in certain areas because, ironically, all the other Jews fled long ago. What other Jews? Those who now reside in "nice" neighborhoods. Those who are wealthier and younger and so much more fortunate. Those who belong to all the Jewish organizations that bleed for every one else. Those liberals who ran away to the safe areas from whence they pontificate to the elderly and poor they left behind: Integrate.

But who cares about these? What Jewish organization is seized by an overwhelming need to hurriedly reorder its priorities so that these elderly Jews may be relocated in other areas? One does not speak of those high-income luxury neighborhoods in which the Jewish Establishment is ensconced. But surely there are apartments in lower middle class neighborhoods where a rent subsidy can grant a poverty-ridden elderly Jew a few last years of safety, Jewish activity, and meaning to his life. But who cares?

More. There are thousands of low-income, Jewish parents who are appalled at the state of the public schools their children attend. Terrified by the physical danger in these schools and frightened at the thought that their children will drift away from Jewish ties, they desperately seek entry for their children into Jewish parochial schools—yeshivas. The latter, choked by inflationary pressures and huge deficits, are forced to charge the kinds of tuition fees that are out of reach of the poor Jewish family. The result is that these needy Jewish children are deprived of the right to a maximum Jewish education and are forced to endure the kind of hell that wealthy Jewish parents' children in the suburban public schools or in the city private schools can escape. But who, among our Jewish Establishment, gives a Jewish damn?

What Jewish group cares enough about this most desperate of Jewish problems, that holds within it the very future of Jewish survival as Jews in America? Who cares enough to see to it that scholarships and tuition subsidies are granted to these poor needy Jewish children so that they might attend a Jewish day school?

The huge federations in Jewish communities have money for all manner of nonsense. Their order of priorities is one that calls for Jewish education to receive the jackal's share of the wealth. They have Jewish funds to give to "Jewish" hospitals whose clientele is predominantly non-Jewish. (Indeed, one of the great puzzles of our time is what makes a hospital "Jewish", particularly when it is not even kosher.) They have Jewish funds to give to summer camps, community centers, and boys' clubs whose participants are so often gentile and which serve, all too often, as convenient places for intermarriage. We have Jewish funds for basketball and basket weaving and all sorts of vapid foolishness, but, for Jewish education—the one thing that will stop the cancer of Jewish alienation, intermarriage, and assimilation—we can find little or no funds.

Indeed, the opposite is true. When the desperate, up-against-the-wall yeshivas finally see some ray of hope, when suddenly the federal and state governments find their way to give money to the secular aspects of the yeshiva curriculum or when they grant tuition subsidies to individual students, those same Jewish groups who sat by and refused to give Jewish money suddenly awake from the dead.

With shouts of moral outrage they come to the aid of the Constitution: Separation of Church and State! Save the Republic! Suddenly the lawyers who cannot be found to go to court for individual Jewish problems descend in hordes to make sure that no government money goes to aid the hard-pressed yeshiva.

It is not strange. The Jewish Establishment is opposed, in principle, to the Jewish yeshiva. It is too Jewish. It is to parochial. It prevents integration of the Jew with the non-Jew. It flies in the face of the First Commandment: Melt. It is a thing to be abhorred. The yeshiva is no friend of the Jewish Establishment, because it reveals its nakedness of Jewish soul and its paucity of Jewish knowledge.

So, who will fight the good Jewish fight and grant the poor Jewish child the means to receive a Jewish education? Who will demand that the Jew get his proper share of antipoverty funds and jobs? Who will help stamp out the hoodlumism and racism that threatens Jews physically? Who will relocate the elderly and poor Jews from the neighborhoods of violence and nightmare? If not the Jew—who? If not the Jewish Establishment whose raison d'être is to aid Jews—who? And if not now, when? And, above all, if Jews do not do these things, why?

There are other Jewish problems about which those who live in the solitude of the gilded ghetto know little, and care less. In Scarsdale or Shaker Heights or Great Neck or Newton or Elkins Park it is pleasant to walk in the streets, the gardens, and the shopping malls. The statistics of manslaughter, mugging, rape, purse snatching, robbery, and burglary have little meaning for the practitioners of the good life.

For Jews in less fortunate circumstances, however, it is not that simple. Such people know the gnawing uncertainty of waiting for a youngster who is late in returning from school. In "nice" areas it is merely a question of whether he went to the home of a friend or

to the library. In other neighborhoods the darkness is a
demon that brings with it fears and trepidations and
where frightened residents see shadows lurking in every
corner. All too often it is not their imagination.

The terror of the streets; the fear that keeps store
doors locked and makes everyone who knocks the subject
of keen scrutiny so as to ascertain whether he is customer
or robber; the vandalizing of synagogues and Jewish
institutions and the attacks upon Jews returning from
them; the robbing of and assaults upon children in public
schools; the breaking into and the ransacking of private
apartments; all these realities are the flesh and blood that
comprise the skeletal stories that the more fortunate only
read of in their daily newspapers. In a word, they make
up the nightmare of crime and violence.

There are neighborhoods throughout the major urban
areas where Jews live in terror of crime and violence. If
one seeks the affirmation of the Biblical curse, "In the
morning thou shalt say, 'Would G-d it were evening!'
and at evening thou shalt say 'Would G-d it were morning'," let him speak to people in these urban neighborhoods whom too many of us never see and whose particular adventures we never experience. The elevator in
an apartment building becomes a dreaded thing and the
dark halls a haven for muggers and worse. The walk to
the synagogue for the evening prayers becomes a rare
event for the frightened Jew, and soon those evening
prayers are delivered to G-d while still daylight in order
that the supplicant arrive home and lock himself in his
caged prison before darkness traps him on the streets.

For the youngster with his skull cap, returning from yeshiva or playing ball in the park, there is the constant physical assault nurtured by the image of the Jew as a weak, frightened easy mark.

The public school for the young Jewish boy becomes a dreaded thing, too, and he learns to control his kidneys because the bathroom has become a place of danger. Extortion of money and food becomes commonplace. Hatred, suspicion, and fear fill the halls of education while a weak and paralyzed principal attempts to keep things quiet lest his record be marred as one who is incapable of keeping things under control. Teachers and administrators both play out each day in grim anticipation of the great moment of retirement.

Merchants leave their homes much the same as peace officers—not totally sure what the day will bring or whether they will not fall victim that day to the robber and dope addict. At best they are certain that the day of assault is eventually due to touch them; at worst they fear that more than their property will be taken. Unable to obtain insurance they sit in their stores warily eyeing those who enter and fearful of pilferage and vandalism.

The Jewish merchant in the non-Jewish ghetto areas fares even worse. His plight grows steadily more desperate, for not only are all the curses that plague other merchants visited upon him with even greater terror, but, in addition, he is the target of extortion, rioting, looting, and burning as well as being the victim of a campaign by local groups to drive him out of their community. The Jew who founded his business and worked long hours and days and years to make it grow; the Jew who was there long before most of the present-day residents had arrived, is the victim of a thinly veiled attempt to drive out all people who are of the wrong ethnic complexion.

And let us remember that many of these Jews who suffer are, so often, the little people. Some are immigrants and survivors of the death camps. Many are owners of neighborhood papa-mama stores who spend long hours trying to save a little money. They, too, seek to climb the same ladder of success as their fellow Jews who now live in nice neighborhoods and who do not care about them.

No one cares about them. Politicians sit and watch the agony of the Jewish victim of crime and prefer not to cause problems by taking the necessary harsh line of defense. Police, with eloquence born of long practice, deliver the line that will some day be engraved mandatorily on the tombstone of every officer: We don't have enough men. It is so much easier to avoid problems by ignoring the cries of the victims. After all, others may riot if dealt with harshly, but Jews, with bitter resignation, accept their lot without a furor . . . .

The Jew can expect precious little help from the wealthy non-Jewish liberal establishment which will always sympathize with the disadvantaged and give them that which is not theirs to give away. They will always be tolerant of those who burn and loot someone else's property. Far better to rob a small Jewish merchant in Harlem than to have acts of violence deflected to the stock exchange or a large Ford Motor dealership. Far

better for Jewish merchants and property owners to suffer than for a mayor who desires to be President to upset
his political ambitions; getting tough with minorities,
who have many more voters, could ruin his image as a
man who keeps things under control. And so no one cares
about the merchants who have been wiped out by arson-
ists on an individual basis or the merchants who have
been hurt by rioters and looters in a general orgy of
destruction. A Jewish merchant can see a lifetime of
work destroyed in a few hours. And no one will care.

If the very reason for the existence of government is
to secure the lives and property of its citizens, then government has failed miserably. If free man long ago made
a social contract with authority whereby he gave up
certain freedoms for the right to be secure—all are agreed
that, for the poor Jew, it was a bad deal. The resident of
the lower income Jewish neighborhoods is subjected to
regular fear of attacks on his body and property. It is not
a pleasant thing. Nor is it a thing that the Jewish organizations have done a thing about.

What Jewish organization has so understood the
terror of the streets, schools, stores, and homes in oppressed Jewish neighborhoods that it has set up an urgent,
well-financed program of safety? What traditional Jewish
group has taken up the cause of Jewish physical safety
with the same zeal and energy that it normally reserves
for non-Jewish social and economic causes? What major
Jewish organization, with its prestigious New York City
upper East Side address and its executives who live in
areas safer than the inner city ones of the little Jew, has

called for mass demonstrations and sent its leaders into the streets with angry protests?

What Jewish leader has decreed that his group will set aside funds for safety patrols so that the people of the neighborhood can have the means to make their streets as safe as those on Long Island? Or in Beverly Hills? What Jewish organization has made the safety of Jewish bodies, synagogues, institutions, streets, schools, stores, and property the subject of major top priority and the recipient of large sums of money? None. And we have an obligation to ask *why?*

With an arrogance and lack of feeling that is unworthy of descendants of Abraham, major Jewish groups have summarily rejected all requests for funds to fight crime with the incredible statement: Go to the police; this is their job. How sublimely ignorant and how obscenely unfeeling! The Jew in the poor and oppressed areas has gone to the police a thousand times and a thousand times he has been left unsatisfied. Perhaps the police in Westchester or Evanston come promptly; in Williamsburg, Crown Heights or Chicago's West Side it takes time, and the hoodlum is rarely found.

And if Jews, without the aid of major Jewish groups, decide on their own initiative to help themselves be safe from murder, rape, and assault, those Jewish leaders who did not feel the obligation to help, lack even the decency not to hurt. The thought of Jewish self-help is inadmissible to them and they make their objections known.

Safety patrols? Vigilantes! Anticrime unit? Violently

taking the law into your own hands! How sad that one who cannot feel someone else's pain should try to prevent the one who does from relieving it. What an orphaned generation we are to be burdened with leaders who say such things and then add: "Furthermore, this is not a Jewish problem; others (read: except us) suffer too."

There are few more outrageous arguments than the one uttered over and over again by Jewish leaders and groups protesting: "Such and such an action is not really a Jewish problem. It is aimed at a class of people which merely includes Jews in their ranks." So we find that assaults on merchants who are predominantly Jewish do not comprise a Jewish issue; that reverse discrimination and quotas that effectively hit Jewish students, businessmen, and workers more than others are not really a "Jewish" problem: that crime in Jewish neighborhoods is not really aimed at the Jew as such and is, therefore, not a "Jewish" problem.

There is irony in these arguments coming from groups and men who, in the Jewish name, take sides on such "Jewish" issues as Vietnam, the Xmas stamp, abortion reform, South Africa, and the electoral college. There is also tragedy. It is the tragedy of lack of sensitivity to Jewish pain, of the de-Judaizing of Jewish problems, of the moral bankruptcy of the Jewish Establishment. If Jews, as part of a general injustice, or general harassment or general persecution, suffer—that *is* a Jewish problem precisely because Jews are involved. Whether *de jure* or *de facto,* it is immaterial to the sensitive Jew, to the one who is consumed by Ahavat Yisroel. The trouble is that our Jewish leaders are assimilated Jews, Jews who have lost touch with the common Jew. They are attempting to subtly melt into the gentile background.

Had they lived in Czarist Russia, they would have stated that the general Russian campaign to Russianize all minorities within their borders—including Poles, Ukrainians, and White Russians as well as Jews—was not a Jewish problem. Woe unto a people with such leaders!

This is not to say that other peoples do not suffer from crime. It is not to say that others do not suffer violence. But for Jewish groups to use this as an excuse not to deal with crime and violence against Jews in Jewish neighborhoods, is inexcusable.

And the fear that flows from this crime and violence into the hearts of the Jews of these stricken neighborhoods becomes a flood of panic. Jews begin to sell their homes and move out of their apartments. They leave their neighborhoods where they lived for years and where they built their lives and gave of their sweat and toil. They flee the place they called home for so long and leave behind all their synagogues, community centers, schools, and institutions that cannot be rebuilt again for tens of millions of dollars. And of course, they leave behind, to the tender mercies of the nightmare of terror, the poor and the elderly who cannot flee.

Who can watch as neighborhoods, hoary with Jewishness and seeping of Jewish history and events, are left to rot? Who does not feel compelled to move to save the Jewish sections with their precious synagogues and institutions that are doomed to be turned into churches, movie houses, or bingo parlors? Who will stop this outrageous plundering of Jewish resources that watches Jewish investments turned into huge losses and sees Jewish communal property sold for a fraction of its value? Who grieves over the losses endured by poor and lower middle class people as their property values plummet and that which they hoped to live in and keep as an investment in their silver years becomes a hideous fiscal joke? Who worries nights over Jewish exoduses that become more frequent and whose moves turn into briefer and briefer pauses to catch their breath before the next Hegira? Certainly not those whose standard of living is so high that their neighborhoods are safe from all the plagues that afflict the poor and middle class.

And then there is the problem of reverse discrimination. It is a fact that, in the name of expiating their own sins, the American establishment has decided to compensate blacks and other minority groups for years of injustice by rewarding them at the expense of the poor and middle class whites. For the Jew this will be disastrous. All that he has gained as a minority, has been gained because of a democratic, competitive merit system. In free and equal competition with others he has been able to win or lose on his own ability and hard efforts. Now, all that is changing.

Now we find ethnic quotas being adopted in schools and employment. Does a college have a small number of minority students or teachers? It does not matter that the small percentage is the result of open and free competition for entry by the attainment of high grades and scholastic ability. Political pressures and fear of trouble by militants dictates that problems be avoided by disregarding merit and going by ethnic quotas. This can doom the Jew. Qualified Jewish high school seniors are denied admittance to first-rate colleges; there is no room for them because a large number of far less qualified minority-group students have been admitted to fulfill the quota. Jewish students are turned down by medical schools while seats are reserved for others who lack the talent but have the "desire." Government scholarships are denied Jews because other groups have preference.

Today, there is preferential treatment, which is a quota system "for" Blacks and Puerto Ricans and Chicanos and which, in itself, guarantees the exclusion of a certain number of qualified Jews. Tomorrow, the quota system will reach its logical conclusion with demands that each nationality and ethnic group be admitted on the basis of the national population percentage and which in effect is "against" a large number of Jews. For a people that makes up only three percent of the American population this is political, economic, and social murder.

And what is true for schools is likewise happening in employment. Quotas for civil service jobs are demanded, and, once again, the Jew is forced out. There are not enough Black, Puerto Rican, or Mexican-American principals? Let the competitive exams be abolished, and hire on the basis of color and ethnic background. More, let the past examinations be disregarded totally or hire, not on the basis of the highest grades, but in alphabetical order. And so we find that Jews who studied long and hard to become administrators, who passed the examinations for these jobs on merit and effort, who waited months and years for an opening to emerge, are suddenly told that they are being overlooked because of the quota system. This is death for the Jews. And what is true for government jobs becomes increasingly true for private industry as preferential treatment is given the minority group member at the expense of someone more qualified—too often, a Jew.

Yet another form of reverse discrimination lies in the demand that persons who are not of the same ethnic or color background of the community be removed as doctors, uniformed officers, or merchants. What is to happen to the Jew if every community follows suit? What will happen will be an economic ghetto into which Jews are squeezed, exactly as they were in Czarist Russia, and a *numerus clausus,* precisely like the one in the Europe they fled. All this in the name of progress and justice.

It is not difficult to understand why government does not protest, and indeed, creates these things. Hoping to divert minority anger, government, usually led by people who are most guilty of persecution of these minorities, attempts to atone for past wrongs by having innocent individuals pay for its sins.

The rich and the powerful American establishment, the Park Avenue and Southampton people, have nothing to lose. Their youngsters will be accepted to the finest schools anyhow. They and their families are not about to compete for teaching, post office, and civil service jobs. It is immensely simple to be liberal with middle-class and lower-class rights. The American establishment is prepared to sacrifice the Jew in order to appease groups that are not as pacific.

What is disheartening is the failure of Jewish organizations to do battle to protest this emasculation of Jewish rights and power. The same groups that find the funds to fight Xmas stamps, state aid to parochial schools, and other issues, do not find the time or the money to fight quotas, or to defend Jewish teachers who have passed merit exams for the position of principal and have been arbitrarily displaced, or to stand up for Jewish students with high grades who have failed to be taken into undergraduate and graduate schools while others with far lower grades have because they are members of more militant minority groups. Once again, we must ask: Why?

Why is it that we cannot get Jewish leaders to see the danger to Jewish survival and fight for us as they fight for others? Why is it that a major Jewish group will go to court to make sure that a wealthy actress will be allowed to buy into a luxury cooperative but will not fight for the poor Jew? Why can we not find Jewish groups who will militantly declare that to take innocent people who are not at fault and to say, "You must pay for the faults of others, . . . " is immoral and unjust. These are innocent people who have done nothing wrong and owe nothing; they should not be forced to pay.

Who will stand up against this potential disaster and proclaim: "A quota system is wrong, because it denies merit. It denies to a person who has worked long and hard the fruits of his labor. Merit implies being color-blind and religion-blind and ethnic-blind and blind to everything except the merits of the person. This is not a question of morality or justice, it is a question of meaningful Jewish progress and survival."

The imposition of a quota system to displace merit will hurt no other group as much as the Jews. We will have suffered twice. We remember the quota system of the past as a horrendous obstacle to obtaining higher education and jobs which our achievements would have otherwise entitled us to. Indeed, the great number of Jewish civil servants is due to past lack of opportunity to become professionals. We remember, too well, the closed doors. They must not be allowed to close again.

It all returns to the original question: Why? Why were we silent thirty years ago, and why are we so timid in our battle for our Soviet Jewish brethren? Why do we fail to mount the proper battle for those Jews who are victims of crime, poverty, and discrimination at home?

Who paralyzed our fraternal reflexes? Why do we not do for ourselves what we do for others? Why do some Jews call and we do not hear? Why do they appeal and we are not there to help? Who murdered Ahavat Yisroel?

THE LOSS OF JEWISH IDENTITY

Once upon a time the Jew came to America. He went to the sweat shops and worked, so that his son might be an American. He peddled, on bitterly cold nights, at Delancey Street and under the hot, dusty, sweaty sun of Rivington, so that his child might see better days as an American. He lived in his roach-ridden and rat-infested tenements at a time when there was little social consciousness to protest his plight, so that his son would be better off than he—as an American. He worked long hours under terrible labor conditions at a time when there were few unions or wages-and-hours laws to stop the exploiters, so that his son might go to school and better himself—as an American. He was determined that his son be educated, even in schools that did not relate to him as a Jew, under teachers who were not community residents and who did not understand him and his background, where the language spoken was not the Yiddish of his home and where there were never enough books or recreational facilities, all so that his son might be able to move up as an American. The good life was not given to the exploited and hardworking Jew of Europe who came here in ship's steerage and lived in tenement steerage and who worked like the Jewish dog that he was, so that his son might be a real American.

The Jew came to America with a Judaism that had survived an exile of twenty centuries. It was his invisible baggage that eluded the customs officials on Ellis Island. He arrived and hastened to build his traditional synagogues where the substance of fervent belief and the reality of tears on Yom Kippur allowed the Almighty to feel at home in His house. He carried over the richness of a difficult but meaningful Sabbath and made sure that his home was sanctified by kosher foods. He continued a traditional Jewish family life that, for centuries, was the envy of the nations.

He was a proud nationalist and felt for each and every Jewish tragedy. Jewishness was a thing to which he related in every fiber of his body and it was this fervent attachment to Judaism and to the Jewish people that helped him to sustain himself in the land of Columbus.

The Jew came to America, one more link in a stubborn chain of centuries, fortified with a faith of deep substance and great moral and spiritual strength. He was imbued with a deep pride in being Jewish and an understanding that he was part of the Jewish people. It was this which had sustained him and his fathers before him in a

Europe where the Czar impressed his eight-year-old child into the army for twenty-five years. It was this which kept him from surrendering when the pogromist sought his body and the Church his soul. It was this which preserved him when the bitter winter sapped his energy and bitterer poverty grasped at his existence.

It was this which now sustained him in his America during days of weary toil and nights of slum-dwelling poverty. It was this which kept him from sinking into the despair of alcohol, the cynicism of rioting, or surrender to hate and moral degradation. The Jew took his Jewishness with him into the streets and the sweat shops where he began the long process of becoming an American. He looked forward to the great Jewish dream—making a life for his son that would be better than the one into which he was born. He dreamed of his son being a fine American and a good Jew.

And that son, gladly and eagerly, gave unto Caesar what was his and then informed his Jewish G-d that He would have to be satisfied with ten cents on the dollar.

It was not that he wanted to totally run away from his Jewish heritage. Raised in a cheder and remembering the old synagogue, unable to forget the Passover Seder and the Sabbath candles and meals, the son of the Jewish immigrant did not seek to destroy Judaism but only to come to an accommodation with it. Live and let live. One thing above all haunted him—the fear of anti-Semitism. He was gripped by the need to do everything to prevent it from harming him in this land, including the Americanization of his Jewishness.

One could continue to be a Jew without wearing his Jewishness on his sleeve. The way to get ahead in America was to understand the reality of the New World and to remember that this was not Poland or Russia or Austria or Turkey. Here, one did not have to be a fanatic about his religion. To flaunt one's Jewishness was to invite anti-Semitism and put up needless barriers to success. In any event, the primary thing about being Jewish was to have a good Jewish heart, to love thy neighbor and to speak about the Ten Commandments.

Accommodations would have to be made and Jewishness would have to adapt itself to the American life-style. If one was fortunate enough to live in a free country he would have to lower his religious barriers. At last, after so many years of persecution, the Jew had an opportunity to live free and he would not throw it away. In America all people were equal and should, as far as possible, minimize their differences. No one could expect the Jew who came to a land of progress and science to retain intact a Judaism and a Jewishness which were parochial and provincial. If one demanded to be treated as all other Americans he could not, at the same time, emphasize too strongly his Jewish differences.

The Jew was prepared to keep his Jewishness but it would have to endure many changes and undergo the proper kinds of revisions. Those rituals which were old-fashioned would have to be discarded and those practices that were too outlandish could not be retained. Jewish identity was important but it could not be too strident; it would have to be muted. One could be a Jew and at the same time not flaunt it; one could be the kind of a Jew that America would not be ashamed of. It was with the knowledge that he could climb the ladder of success in America, with determination to do so and with a wariness of anything that might hinder him, that the son of a wandering Jew created his brand of American Jewishness.

That son, raised in a Yiddish home, where prayers were given to G-d in an un-American tongue and where customs were foreign to these American shores; that son whose parents' accent grated on his hard-earned American ear and whose father's lack of *savoir faire* made one who wished to enter the mainstream so uncomfortable; that son whose demanding religion was too much of a burden in a modern America and whose Jewishness was such a yoke on a Sammy who wanted so much to run— that son determined to grow up to be a real American. He succeeded mightily in that—and more. He grew up to be that mighty force—the American Occasional Jew.

He became the Jew driven by insecurity and doubts to show the gentile that he was as good as he. He became the one pushed by great need to be accepted and by fearful complexes to be loved, or at least tolerated. He was the Jew who proclaimed his equality but was forever looking over his shoulder to see if the anti-Semite was there. It was not enough for him to discard his beard and his unfashionable clothing, he had to throw off his embarrassing Judaism. One cannot take a man into the New World without ridding him of the Old World inferiority, and the first-generation son of the laboring zeyde carried his albatross around his circumcised neck. It consisted of his embarrassment with his "antiquated" faith, his fear of what the gentile might think of his medieval and so-very-strange differences, his distaste for anything that might link him to a foreign, too-Jewish past. And so the hater of Jewish fanaticism became a fanatic in his efforts to escape.

He took Jewish substance and traded it for a bagels-and-lox Judaism. (Do not believe the one who cries that he is a "Jew at heart"; American Judaism is based on the intestines.) He took a synagogue inhabited by Heaven and substituted for it a Jewish Center run by a caterer. In his self-inferiority and vague sense of shame he cast away the tradition of a meaningful, disciplined Jacob and became an American Esau—selling his magnificent birth-right for the lentils of the American good life.

The hatred and contempt manifested by the anti-Semite is an attempt to degrade the Jew. It is an effort to instill within him a feeling of inferiority. In the case of the American Jew, it succeeded too often.

Too often, running Sammy seemingly believed the anti-Semite. Too often he agreed to his scheme to promote self-hatred and shame with subsequent attempts to escape his Jewishness. Those who changed their too-Jewish sounding names; those who gave their children exotically WASP-sounding Christian names; those who cringed at the sight of a bearded Hassid; those who attempted to change their religious practices so that they might be more in line with accepted practice; those who shrank from militant Jewish defense of their rights and, of course, those who chose to escape from Jewishness totally whether through religious conversion, through total lack of identification with anything Jewish, or through revolutionary internationalism — all these succumbed to the efforts of the anti-Semite. All buried Jewish pride and raised high the flag of retreat from too-militant Jewish identity. All hoped to escape gentile Jew-hatred by adopting a Jewish kind of self-hatred.

In his sophistication, Sammy scorned much of his Jewish past and consigned it to the trash can of historical obscurantism. And having done that, the modern and analytical American Jew proceeded to build his own myths. They were all aimed at eradicating anti-Semitism, at gaining security and peace of mind. Nevertheless, they remained myths.

He put his trust in the Melting Pot, that great and wondrous myth that the Jew elevated to an article of faith. A society that melted meant a society where the Jew would not be different or singled out for persecution. Weary of his persecution and anxious to throw off his two-thousand-year-old agony, the American Jew yearned to melt.

Melt! This was the new Categorical Imperative. Melt! This was the way to assimilate properly and with honor, with none of the gnawing pangs of conscience that accompanied the European form of escape from Jewishness — conversion. Melt! Was there a happier concept for one whose goal in life was to make it? Melting meant the blurring of distinctions. Melting was the great equalitarian credo of the frantic American Jew.

"Hear O Israel, America is our G-d; America is the land of One."

In the Melting Pot, all stewed together. In the Melting Pot, there was an indivisibility that forever hid the Jew as a distinct entity to be attacked. There was light at the end of the long tunnel of exile and the directions to that nirvana read: Melt! This was the way to abolish Jew-hatred. Melt! The Jew now had to do his part, to make sure that America marched forward resolutely with pot in hand.

And so he put his faith, did this panting Sammy, in such things as Education which he saw as the key to his own freedom and security. Surely, he told himself, if only enlightenment could flood man's dull minds the millennium would be upon us. Who could doubt that a sheepskin in every pot and a Phi Beta Kappa key on every vest would banish forever the bigotry and prejudice that so haunted the Jew? For it was clear to any Sammy who had eyes to see that hate, bias, pogroms, and holocausts were the products of ignorance and that if the muses could only kiss the brows of Neanderthal man, sweetness and light would be upon us to banish forever into the recesses of history the darkness of ignorance and intolerance. This was the way to abolish Jew-hatred. This was the way to melt.

And so he put his faith in Liberalism. Only the unenlightened failed to understand that it was dire poverty and disadvantage that created the demons of discontent who brought forth the terror of Jew-hatred. Surely, if one backed the cause of the oppressed they would embrace us in their gratitude and, once raised to the level of equality, would march with us in a brave new world. And so the eager Jew rushed forward to do battle for all causes in a mad haste to stand at the head of the crusading line. Equality for oppressed peoples would mean security for the Jew—thus spake the American Jew. This was the way to abolish Jew-hatred. This was the way to melt.

And so he put his faith in Equality, that great leveler, and he insisted that all people be equal and all differences be erased. What surer way for the Jew to be accepted than if he and all others were equally equal? How could anti-Semitism possibly exist in a society that melted all differences and molded all into one indistinct shape? Equalize! This was the way to abolish Jew-hatred. This was the way to melt.

And so he put his faith in Democracy. Was it not clear beyond a shadow of a doubt that it was tyranny alone that begat all the evils that had afflicted us and that the masses, the "people," were possessed of a mystical ability to ascertain truth? If only granted the opportunity, if only given the vote, if only allowed to let their voices be heard—the people would inevitably reject hatred, tyranny, fraud, and falsehood and would somehow achieve Truth. Free elections would find the people opting for goodness and freedom and sanity. Free elections and Democracy were the way to abolish Jew-hatred. This was the way to melt.

And so he put his faith in Secularism. The Jew who had once been the essence of all that was spiritual, now became the spokesman for Secularism. He who had survived on Earth by his stubborn faith in Heaven now became the crusader for the Great Wall of America —that which separated Church and State. If a Xmas tree was contemplated on some mid-western township's official lawn, vigilance on the part of the Secularist knocked it down. If the United States government contemplated a stamp with a religious motif, it would have to be done away with. If parochial schools faced bankruptcy, no state aid dared be contemplated, for Religion was the great divider and one could not melt when Church—and Synagogue—insisted on Identity. It was the public school that had to be defended at all costs because it was the public schools that stood for all that melted.

Parochial schools stood for Identity, hence, division, and no one fought harder against his own parochial schools than the emancipated Jew. In yeshivas one met only "one's own kind" and this was against all the theory of "Melt." Religion had to be neutralized and Secularism raised on high whether people liked it or not. This was the way to abolish Jew-hatred. This was the way to melt.

And so he put his faith in Materialism. If only one could give the masses enough to eat and drink; if only they had their cars to ride about in and their television sets to stupefy themselves with; if only one could satisfy dissatisfaction, surely there would be no bitterness and no envy and no rebellion—and no anti-Semitism. Gone was the idea of Man being a spiritual creation, and embraced was the concept of Man as a higher animal.

Satisfy his cravings and he will be content. Soothe his lusts and he will lay himself down to sleep. People hated Jews because they were poor; give them wealth and all would be well. Those who created Miami Beach and the Catskill resorts understandably looked upon bread and circuses as salvation and predictably conceived such answers. This was the way to abolish Jew-hatred. This was the way to melt.

And so he put his faith in Love. If only people would love everyone else and bury hate, how safe the world would be for all peoples—and how little anti-Semitism there would be around. And so he made sure to love everyone else and to march for any cause that raised its head. How noble to march for civil rights! He marched for civil rights and for Republican Spain and for the oppressed everywhere so that Love might come to the world and make it safer for all—including the Jew. He opened his synagogues to Christians so as to prove to them that all that they had heard about him was false. See, he beamed as he led them about, we are a people who really do not use Christian blood on Passover and who never would have dreamed of crucifixions. Indeed we love you—and will you not love us, too? And he crusaded for interfaith services, and his rabbis exchanged pulpits with those ministers who cared to, and he sat in his pew glowing with acceptance as the Right Reverend deigned to grace the Temple pulpit. This was the way to abolish Jew-hatred. This was the way to melt.

So he put his faith in Public Relations, and his organ-

izations ground out rivers of material aimed at pro-
moting "tolerance" and "understanding." His Christian
neighbor was bombarded with literature explaining—in
sophisticated fashion—that Jews really had neither horns
nor tails. And so his synagogues became Jewish Centers,
and his Centers begat Temples, and they were huge,
massive, incredibly expensive architectural creations
which found the Diety wandering about lost, attempting
in vain to find the Sanctuary. It was not strange since
they were built not for Heaven but to impress the earthy
gentile. This was the way to melt.

Above all, he paid homage to Respectability. It was
of paramount importance that the Jew did not say or
do things that might provoke non-Jews and inflame Jew-
hatred. The image of the Jew was vital, and irresponsible and too-militant words and deeds were liable to
upset all that the Jew had worked for, so long and hard.
One had to be part of the general mainstream and not
do things that might outrage the general American public. What one said was important, and how he said it
even more so. Of course, Jews were as equal as everyone else and as secure as all others, nevertheless, being
looked upon favorably was all-important and the Jew
was ever watchful of his public Ps and Qs. This was
the way to melt.

And some put their faith in Internationalism and
looked forward to abolishing national boundaries and
religious and ethnic distinctions. For what better way
to do away with anti-Jewishness than to have no Jews
left to be anti? Let no more the divisive national an-

thems of the world be heard, and let the invidious flags and banners be cast away. And so some rejected Zionism and *Hatikva* and turned to the *Internationale* and the Red Flag; some spat on fellow Jews and embraced the world's proletariat. This was their way to abolish Jew-hatred. This was their way to melt.

All this to bury, once and for all, Jew-hatred.

This is the "Torah" that our Establishment Moses'es have placed before the American Children of Israel. These were the principles of faith of the American Jew. They were designed to assure his safety, security, and salvation. They were created to end anti-Semitism. The results were predictable.

The briefest perusal of them reveals a common denominator: All must, in the end, modify and mute the strong, Maximalist Jewish tradition of an indivisible Jewish people with first loyalties one to the other, with deep and emotional Jewish pride and nationalism. All are designed to replace intense and powerful Jewish pride and nationalism with their very antithesis, with the principle of Melt.

To *melt* means to ignore differences and to integrate with those about you. Jewish nationalism and pride, on the other hand, declare that, while one lives at peace and in friendship with his neighbors, he emphasizes the uniqueness and differences of his Jewishness and knows that there exists from Jew to Jew a love and obligation that is unique. All the Jewish marchings for every liberal and social cause were designed to knock down the barriers between peoples but they also weakened Jewish ties to themselves. All the Jewish drives for ecumenism were meant to show how little difference there was between religions; they also diluted the particularism of their own faith.

What the Jew originally set out to do was to prove to the gentile that a Jew was no different than anyone else. In the end, he succeeded in convincing himself. In such a setting, Jewish pride becomes a pale and unconvincing thing and Jewish nationalism a contradiction to all the love and brotherhood the Jew and his leaders are propagating. It is impossible to retain the strong and emotional Jewish national concept of Ahavat Yisroel —love of Jews—in the face of a Jewish drive to melt. It is too much to expect specific Jewish pride to survive an atmosphere of integration, amalgamation, equality of all, world brotherhood, and the need to fight for all causes as if they were our own. With such goals there can be no intense feeling of oneness and no special closeness to a Jew who is in pain. As Liberalism, Equality and Secularism make all men the same why should the Jew feel a special obligation to aid a second Jew? As maximum Jewish education is laid to rest, from whence shall come Jewish pride and identity? The Jew becomes a man of the world, a humanist, and is not particularly concerned about Jewish problems as such. The plight of the Jew in the Soviet Union may be disturbing but so is that of the oppressed Ethiopian. Jews in the urban areas are poor, old, and the victims of violence? True, but so are others. The Jew in Brooklyn has problems? Of what concern is that to the one who lives in Great

Neck? "Let the urban Jew solve his own problems; I have my own."

Why is there no concerted and emotional Jewish drive to aid a fellow Jew? Why are there no huge crowds to protest on behalf of Jews? The answer is that the wellsprings of Jewish brotherhood and nationalism run dry when we cut off their exclusive sources, and apathy and selfishness grow in proportion to the death of Jewish pride and nationalism. Who murdered Ahavat Yisroel, the love of one Jew to another Jew, the looking upon each and every Jew as a brother and sister, the feeling of Jewish pain as if it were our own? We did; we and our leaders who sought safety from Jew-hatred in the principle of Melt.

And there is yet another reason. One who is obsessed with preserving himself will, of necessity, find that the bonds that link him to a fellow Jew become weaker. The more concerned we are with surviving our own narrow plight, the less capable we are of feeling the pain of others. It is not that we do not care about our brother; it is that we care more about ourselves, and we begin to measure each crisis in terms of what it means for us. We begin to weigh all our actions carefully to be absolutely sure that we are not endangered. We become cautious about becoming involved. What will it mean for my job? What will my family say? How will it affect me socially? And the standard of all standards: What will "they" say?

Of all the myths, none is more fervently feared and believed than that of Respectability. If only the Jew is respectable and responsible and does not rock any boats, he will not awaken the sleeping demon of Jew-hatred. Of all the American Jewish sacred cows and of all the golden calves at whose altars we worship, none is as awesome as Respectability. Respectability! If all the respectable Jewish organizations were laid end to end, there would be no end to them. In weighing the question of whether Jews should do certain things, and in analyzing how these things should be done, the yardstick and the measuring rod invariably are: What will "they" think?

We do not seek to find that path which will be of the most immediate and permanent benefit to Jews, because, all too often, such things are "improper," "un-Jewish," and "dangerous." Some things disturb us because they may improperly disturb "them." What will "they" think? How will "they" react to Jewish conduct that is unorthodox? That is what obsesses us; that is what destroys us.

My grandfather, of blessed memory, was a man who was learned, pious, and well beloved by all the people in the town of Safed, Israel. He was, in short, graced with all the finest of attributes. There was only one slight failing that he had—and it was this that kept his family from being wealthy.

My grandfather, you see, was a man who was quite worried about what people thought. "Mah yomru habriyos?" (What will the people say?) was a general rule that he followed, and it really did cost him a great deal. The story? Here it is.

The Land of Israel, at the turn of the century, lay beneath the heel of the Sick Man of Europe, the Ottoman Turk. Approximately fifty thousand Jews lived there; concentrated in Jerusalem, Safed, Hebron, and Tiberias. They were poor, generally living off the halukah (charity) that was collected in Eastern Europe. They were almost all observant Jews with only a handful of secularists, young intellectuals who called themselves Zionists, hacking away at the malarial land and swamps.

Safed, the city of Cabala, where Rabbi Yitzchak Luria and Joseph Karo had lived, held a population of twelve thousand Jews who eked out a bare living, but who luxuriated in the spiritual holiness of the Land of Israel. My grandfather was one of those rare Safed Jews who was a businessman. His cronies were mostly people who would gather at the Sanzer Midrash, the study hall and synagogue built by the followers of the Rabbi of Sanz. There, they would talk politics, religion, G-d, and whatever else they might care to dissect, including every inhabitant of Safed. Perhaps it was the fear of falling into the worldly clutches of the Safed loiterers that made my grandfather wary of doing anything without first making a mental note: What will the people say?

And so, one day, my grandfather rose early in the morning and set off on a business trip. He was gone all day and returned just in time for the late afternoon prayer at the synagogue. Naturally, the loafers gathered about to find out where he had gone, what he had done, and in short, all that had transpired so that they might pass judgment upon it.

It so happened that my grandfather had gone to a small, backwater village on the coast, far from Jewish habitation. There he had bought some land in the center of the village along the seashore. When the "experts" heard what my grandfather had done they raised a unanimous cry of mixed mockery and anguish: "Are you crazy, Reb Nachman! Since when does a Jew throw away his money on a foolish business venture such as this? You have been swindled; the land is worthless!"

My grandfather was really quite a good businessman and he believed that the land had great speculative value. But the old bogey reared its ugly head. The "people" had spoken; the "people" had laughed and called it a foolish thing. He quickly rescinded the deal.

Now, I have seen poor people and seen rich people, and, while it may not always be true, it seems to me that it may be better to be rich. The reason that my grandfather died a poor man may be that the little backwater village he had visited was named Haifa and the land he had bought was a good share of what is now that city's port.

What happened as the result of my grandfather's obsession with public opinion was hardly earthshaking. We survived. What happens when Jewish leaders and the Jewish public become so fearful at what "they" will say that they become paralyzed into inactivity, can be tragically fatal.

Why were we silent? Why do our organizations condemn Jewish militants today? Why were *the very same groups* stricken with political laryngitis as millions died at Auschwitz?

The answer to that is our shame and disgrace. Our Jewish leaders refused to call us into the streets and closed their mouths and hearts because they feared that too strident a protest and too militant a demonstration would lead "them"—the non-Jews of America—to look upon the war as a "Jewish war." In a word, *they* might become anti-Semitic; *our* position in the United States might become worse. We shuddered at the thought. We shut our mouths; we sealed our hearts. The Jews of Auschwitz died.

What would "they" say? "They" were, of course, the non-Jews. "They" were the ones who obsessed our timid Jewish leaders. Would "they" be upset as Jews marched and fought for slaughtered brothers and sisters? Would this lead to anti-Semitism? How would *we* be affected and how would these militant Jewish actions threaten *our* comfortable lives by their too-too Jewishness?

And that which stained Jewish honor thirty years ago is being repeated today. The Jewish Establishment looks at its wealth and position and prestige and—in immense insecurity—wonders what will happen to all of it if we protest too vigorously on behalf of Soviet Jewry.

Has there ever really been as loud a hue and cry about Jewish "terrorism" and "irresponsibility" as we have heard in recent times? Surely not since the very same people who are so hysterical today were condemning other Jewish terrorists and hoodlums twenty-five years ago. In case we have forgotten, the terrorists of a generation ago were called the Irgun and Sternists. The more Jewish history moves forward, the more it gets nowhere; the more we should learn, the surer we may be that we will repeat our stupidities.

Does one really think it is only fear for Soviet Jews that leads Jewish leaders to foam at the mouth? Do we really think that what causes certain groups to roll about in agony and urge the President of the United States to catch the "bad" Jews, is their deep love for the Jews of the Soviet Union? If tender love for the Jews of the USSR gripped these groups, they might, at least, have held *one* street protest rally for Soviet Jews from 1917 to 1963. If sleepless nights over the fate of Soviet Jewry possessed our leaders, they would have simply called the Jewish militants and asked for just *one* meeting with them to discuss the problem.

It is not so much concern for Soviet Jewry that drives our Establishment up the wall. It is the old, pathetic insecurity born of the galut mentality. It is the whispered anguish: What will "they" say?

If there are angry and frightened yelps when Jews form defense patrols in frightened and crime-ridden Jewish urban areas to protect the poor and the elderly residents, if young Jews who daily run the gauntlet of anti-Semitic gangs are taught the art of fighting back (and rather well, at that) if all the respectable, comfortable, and unthreatened rise up in anger and cry "vigilantism" or "hoodlumism," let it be known that their concern is for their own status and position. Let it be known that as they protest they look over their shoulders at "them."

Chain ourselves to the White House gates to attempt to save Holocaust Jews? Sit in the streets for Soviet Jewry? Teach young Jews to be tough and to hit back at their oppressors? Form self-defense units to protect elderly Jews in crime-ridden neighborhoods? This is no way for nice Jewish boys to behave. This is not the way of the respectable Jew. This is not the way to be accepted by our non-Jewish neighbors.

And so we attempt to acquire a low profile and measure each of our actions by anticipating the reactions of others and wondering whether our own position will be damaged and our own reputations sullied. We are frightened people, and we allow our fright to paralyze our actions on behalf of our people. In our fear of making things worse for ourselves we allow things to be much, much worse for other Jews.

We have allowed the concept of Ahavat Yisroel to petrify, and we ourselves have become immune to others' pain, and we fail to hear the cry of our brethren. Like some resurrected Cain, we reply to the question "Where is your brother?" with the retort "Am I my brother's keeper?"

But surely we are, and if his cries are unheard we are surely as doomed as Cain was and will carry on our foreheads that mark of unfeeling selfishness that must, in the end, lead to our own destruction. That destruction will come from an erosion of our Jewish soul and spirit;

that destruction will culminate in a physical holocaust. For no Jew who refuses to move on behalf of his brother can hope to survive the anger of Heaven that demands, above all, the militant fellowship of our people.

Many centuries ago there lived a Jewish daughter named Esther. She was a queen and she was able to escape the sufferings and persecutions endured by others of her people. And when a decree was handed down "to murder and exterminate" the Jews of the empire, she hesitated when asked to intervene with the king, because of the danger involved for herself. And as she hesitated, Mordechai spoke to her, and his words thunder through the ages for all of us to hear:

"Think not with thyself that thou shalt escape in the king's house, more than all the Jews. For if thou holdest thy peace at this time then shall enlargement and deliverance arise to the Jews from another place but thou and thy father's house shall be destroyed: And who knoweth whether thou art not come to the kingdom for such a time as this?"

But it is difficult to argue with fear and with insecurity. Respectability is the last refuge of a frightened Jew. It stems from his fear of anti-Semitism and has its roots in insecurity, doubts of the future, and suspicion of his true position in non-Jewish society. These fears and tensions lead the Jew to weigh each and every word and deed on the nervous scale of the opinion of the non-Jew. The need to win the approval of the non-Jew leads the frightened Jew to do those things we think they will like and to refrain from those things they will oppose. Such a conduct requires a constant survey of what is acceptable and what is not. It leads to a paralysis of will and action. Though we know that we should behave a certain way for the good of another Jew or for his survival we refrain from acting because we are paralyzed by its lack of respectability. We refrain from doing the correct Jewish thing because we are lashed to the stake of Respectability.

Such is the way of disaster for the Jew. Such is the antithesis of Ahavat Yisroel, which places the good of a fellow Jew over all other considerations. Respectability that is born of fear of the non-Jew and absorption with our own security will mark the death-knell of the Jew. Already it has claimed too many victims. Such Respectability must be buried before it buries us.

THE ANTI-SEMITES

From his insecurity and fears, from his obsession with those who hated him and his frantic need to escape that hate, the Jew groped to build for himself a brave new world standing on all the above-named foundations. He begat leaders who took an oath on these principles. He chose rabbis who would swear fealty to them. And as the years passed, a Jewish Establishment grew up, strong, fat, and entrenched, that worshipped hourly at the altar of Melt and that led its flock into green pastures. Yea, though we walked through the Valley of Exile, we had no need to fear, for our Establishment assured us that all was well. If only we melted and if only our Judaism was properly modified and if only our Jewishness was properly muted we would be safe and secure and would dwell in the House of America forevermore.

Of course, there were ignorant people across the land who still mouthed nasty things concerning Jews. The proper thing, we were told, was to ignore them. One did not sink to the level of a bigot by returning his attacks. To be sure, Jew-hatred was not totally eradicated, but the incidents that we read about in the newspapers were better left ignored since attention to them would merely exacerbate the situation. Paying too much attention to minor incidents would only play into the hands of the haters and make things worse. If there appeared to be a growth of anti-Jewish incidents it was merely because we were too unsophisticated to recognize their origin.

And so, we put our faith in Disregarding. We disregarded "minor" incidents of Jew-hatred. We ignored "unimportant" cases of attacks on Jews. We paid no attention to the ravings of a few demented, lunatic-fringe groups "who in no way represent American thinking." Believe us, the Jew was told by his leaders, the proper answer to anti-Semitism is study and not paranoid militant action. The future is bright, the horizons clear. Believe us, American Jews—the Establishment told us from their spacious offices and Melting Pot addresses—believe us that Jew-hatred is on the wane, dying, and everything is beautiful.

And the Jew believed. He believed in the principles of Melt with the same fervor that his antiquated zeyde had once believed in the thirteen Principles of Faith. He believed, he believed.

He believed that all would be good—because he

wanted so much to believe. He believed that Jew-hatred
was a dying thing—because he needed to believe. He
saw what he wished to see and heard what he wished
to hear and believed what he wished to believe—because
it was too painful to do anything else. He saw a move
toward ecumenism on the part of certain intellectual
churchmen and read into it an end to religious hatred
of the Jew. He found wealthy Jews able to buy coopera-
tives that were formerly verboten and Jewish executives
moving into corporate complexes that were once Juden-
rein and believed that this was a permanent sign of the
times. Jewish organizations ran polls that asked whether
the person queried liked Jews and announced that anti-
Semitism was dying. More and more, clubs took in exclusive Jews, and the Jew likened this to the parting
of the Red Sea. Jewish leaders told him that an American version of the Messiah was on his way in his white
sportscar, and he believed. How sweet it was to believe.

He believed and counted his assets, and, behold, they
were many. He numbered his wealth and found that he
had succeeded beyond his fondest dreams. He had
achieved the good life, an his home lay fat and mortgaged on the green lawns of suburbia. His wife was
sleek and happy in her fashionable clothes (that took
so much of his income and health to produce) and her
free time and her mahjong and bingo and cards and
PTAs and all the things that marked the good life. Above
all, anti-Semitism, if not dead, was dying and the Jew
was accepted in all parts of society. He could gamble
in Las Vegas and get drunk in Miami Beach and watch

the horses run at Hialeah. Let us give thanks to the Lord, for He is good, for Jew-hatred is on the wane and everything is beautiful.

It is not true. The Golden Land is *not* as glittering as we would wish to believe and the best laid plans of mouse-like men usually go awry. The vision of an America which would slay the dragon of Jew-hatred and the ideal of a land of the permanent Jewish Nirvana have proven to be somewhat less than that.

We see what we wish to see. We believe what we wish to believe. The myth of a melting pot and of honorable and subtle Jewish assimilation and escape into a Land of the Free and Home of the Brave has been shattered a thousand times over in the past decade. Our leaders assured us and we were misled; it is time for an age of maturity and honest soul searching. The reality that is the American Jewish present and the specter that is the American Jewish future must be looked at, with the proper amount of honest agony.

For the American Jew, nurtured on sweet myths and happy illusions, it is not easy. Children love candy, and that is understandable. Foolish adults do, too, and that is dangerous.

Children of all ages gravitate toward pleasantries and happy thoughts regardless of their validity or truth. It is infinitely better to dream happy things than to face unpleasant reality. We avoid the dentist's drill in the delusion that, somehow, the cavity will go away. The price we pay, in the end, is the tooth. We prefer to ignore that which upsets us, with the rationalization that it will somehow disappear of its own volition. That which is upsetting is better ignored, and that which is unpleasant is better buried from consciousness. Such is the way of the child, the immature adult, and the American Jew.

As the child ripens into manhood his good sense and maturing mind should reject such thinking as silly and dangerous foolishness. The truth, however, is that man usually limits his growth to the physical, retaining his immaturity and clinging to weakness much as does the growing child who cannot bear to be parted from a friendly blanket. The pleasure-pain principle is a strong one and we prefer to put off the unpleasant for tomorrow and tomorrow and tomorrow—until the next tomorrow is too late.

Such is the way of Man, and the Jew is like all other men—but much more so. Beaten and lashed, persecuted and destroyed, he will not listen to that which is unbearable. Over the centuries of holocaust he has built for himself a defense mechanism that blots out horror. He believes in political magic. He desires to see illusions and prefers to disregard the cold chill of reality. Our need to escape painful decisions causes us to create mirages and surely to believe in those that others have built for us. It causes us to see lambs where lions roam and hope where blackness reigns. Since we live in the affluent society and since our insecurity grows in proportion to our wealth, we seek desperately to cling to the good life and refuse to make the immediate sacrifices needed to survive. We pretend that the danger will go away without effort on our part, and we substitute closed eyes for open minds.

'Twas ever thus. Adolf Hitler wrote a book and, in it, precisely detailed how he would gouge and maim human decency. Our illusions grew in proportion to his carrying out of his blueprint; our paralysis grew in proportion to our illusions. It is said that the residents of the Warsaw ghetto, hardly strangers to the realities of Nazi bestiality, refused, for two years, to believe that the trainloads of Jews exported weekly to the country-side were going to the extermination camps despite all the tragic evidence to the contrary. That which is too terrible to contemplate is easier overlooked, misinterpreted and consigned to blessed oblivion.

The great Zionist leader Zev Jabotinsky describes a conversation he once had with Dr. Max Nordau, the Zionist companion of Theodore Herzl in the creation of the movement for a Jewish state. He spoke to him of the immediate necessity of Jewish action to attain their homeland and asked how it was possible for the Jews to stand by and do nothing.

The white-haired Nordau, veteran of a thousand experiences in dealing with his people, replied:

"The Jew learns not by way of reason but from catastrophes. He won't buy an umbrella merely because he sees clouds in the sky; he waits until he is drenched and catches pneumonia—then he makes up his mind."

The result of Jewish self-delusion is always tragedy. Threats do not go away by being ignored—they, rather, become worse. Problems do not disappear merely because we prefer not to think of them; they become aggravated.

"Who is wise?" our rabbis ask; "He who foresees the future," and by this they mean, he who is willing to face the future, who is not afraid to grapple with terrible reality, who meets the problem before it becomes crisis, and who grapples with crisis before it becomes tragedy. In our times such men are not only wise; in an era where there are too few men, such a man is also courageous.

In these days, we are doubly cursed. It is not only that there are too few who are mature enough to face ugly reality rather than slinking into happy illusion, but these are the days when the pygmies of the spirit lash out at those who *do* grapple with reality. Those who warn of impending tragedy are greeted with scornful cries of "paranoia." Those who insist that their fellows stop ignoring reality are castigated and smeared. A Jeremiah is never popular and Cassandra is always feared, but for the Jew in our times such a thing can spell destruction.

It is bad enough when the individual Jew is a victim of his own immaturity. It is catastrophic when Jewish leadership joins him in myopia and in slashing assaults on those who cry out for sanity and vigilance. For it is the leader who reassures the individual Jew in his false security; it is the Jewish organization which comforts him in his blindness and thus assures his failure to prepare for impending tragedy.

Let it be known and shouted from the Jewish roof tops. The Golden Land is not as golden as yesterday, and yesterday was not as golden as the day before. Worse—it is clear that tomorrow will not be as golden as today, while after that . . .

The abatement of open Jew-hatred that we have observed over the past twenty-five years was not a result of our efforts to make ourselves loved. It was not due to the success of our efforts to Melt. It was not because of Democracy or Equality or Liberalism or Secularism. It was not a victory for our Public Relations and ecumenical materials that "proved" that Jews are really good people. There has been no basic change in the dislike of vast numbers of people for the Jew, and the insecurity of the Diaspora remains unchanged. The cause of the apparent New Eden for American Jewry was a result of two things—both most temporary.

The terrible Holocaust that shocked the world with its horrors created a temporary embargo on anti-Semitism. Following a particularly horrible disaster the Jew can always expect world sympathy. 'Twas ever thus. Each pogrom brought forth shock and backing for the Jew; the Jew buys his world opinion with bodies. It was the destruction of six million Jews that made the anti-Semitist a temporary pariah.

Added to this was the unprecedented economic boom that saw most Americans abruptly able to participate in the good life. Suddenly, jobs were plentiful for almost everyone and large numbers of members of the lower classes were able to buy their own homes, acquire their own automobiles, stare at their own television sets, and wallow in the materialism that they had never had before. When people are swimming in the waters of consumer goods, active hatred of Jews is not the thing that is uppermost on their minds. Those who pander to our basest emotions and those groups who thrive on racism and hatred have lean pickings during economic booms. A steak in the broiler and a sleek new car in the garage tend to dilute the appeal of the demagogue. Anti-Semitism in the post World War II period floundered on the rocks of good times and the guilt of Auschwitz.

But this, in no way, means that the basic cancer of Jew-hatred has been eradicated. A disease arrested is not a disease eliminated. And things have begun to change. The disease has begun to appear more brazenly and more threateningly, the rodents have begun to come out of their holes and from under the rocks.

America is, today, a troubled land. Torn by racial passion and hatreds, millions of citizens watch, with mounting anger and frustration, such issues as the busing of their children to other schools for the purposes of an integration most do not want and many fear. Neighborhoods that were formerly all-white now begin to change, and opposition leads to bitterness and hate. Competition for blue-collar and certain low-level white-collar jobs suddenly appears, for the first time in the form of black faces. The white worker, threatened, grows tense and prepares to fight. It is not a pleasant thing and not a good thing, but to ignore its existence is to court disaster.

Not a week goes by that we do not hear of racial clashes and tensions in schools or in the armed forces.

The fact that cities are not burning, the increase in the number of black mayors and other public officials and the growth of minority opportunity foster within us an illusion of progress and a cooling of tensions. But this is a false hope. Perhaps this very growth of minority political and economic growth guarantees that things will be worse. For the minorities, there is a rise in expectations and a growth of impatience with the past pace of progress. For the white, the growing strength of minorities is proof that his own status and position is threatened, thus driving him into a corner of fear and apprehension. When the real bread and butter issue—the competition between blacks and whites for jobs—becomes acute, all the racial tensions that have lain just beneath the surface will come bubbling up.

And who will be blamed? Surely, the Jew. Surely, there will be thrown up to him his leadership, guidance, financial, and physical help to the civil rights movement. All the things that were derived from the Jewish moral and ethical instinct and from his sacred mythical belief that Liberalism, Equality, and Justice for others would bring him his own freedom, will come crashing down about his head.

All the white ethnic groups—the Italians, the Poles, the Irish, the Germans, the Lithuanians, the low-income Anglos—all these who never did melt despite the Jewish Midsummer Night's Dream—will arise and turn upon the Jew. It will be difficult for the Jew to understand, for was he not doing only what is right and just? But it is not the Jew who is the blue-collar worker and the one most immediately threatened by economic competition. He cannot understand that, when it is a matter of direct challenge, few people practice what they can so easily preach when civil rights is a distant ideology. The only one who will sympathize with the Jew will be the upper-class WASP grateful to see both blacks and poorer whites turn on the Jew instead of on himself.

The war in Southeast Asia, with its domestic poisoning of relations between young and old, liberals and conservatives, has aggravated a social gap now widened into a chasm of generations and social classes. Changing values and a changing world find millions of Americans shocked and unable to understand or to cope. The result is a potential reaction and explosion.

The country is torn apart by groups with totally different values, each unable and unwilling to understand the other. Each mistrusts the other. Each feels threatened by the other. And in this setting, the war, which served as the focus of this discontent and difference, this explosion of changing and differing values, assumes a terrible danger for the Jew.

The war has been a defeat for the United States. There is no doubt that this defeat came about not on the battlefield but through the tremendously successful efforts of the antiwar movement. That defeat is already being used to lay the groundwork for a reaction against democracy, dissent and—the Jew. The humiliation in Southeast Asia is focused against a general U.S. loss of prestige throughout the world and growing resentment of this on the part of an officer corps, maligned.

As the Weimar Republic fell before a legend of a Germany stabbed in the back by traitors at home, so is there being woven today a myth of hatred and fascist tyranny that blames the Jew. Standing in the forefront of the peace movement were a great many Jews, most sincerely opposed to a war that they regarded as immoral and unnecessary. Their names were headlined, and long after all the gentile names are forgotten, it is the Jewish ones that remain embedded in the minds of too many Americans who, angry and bitter, seek a devil to blame.

When some of those Jewish names are linked with the radical and fascist Left movement, it merely served to convince frightened America of the Jewish "menace." For the rise of this reckless, stupid Left, with its calls for revolution and the overthrow of an ordered society that most Americans cherish, posed a chilling threat to citizens of middle America. Tens of millions of these Americans have been terrified by the excesses of unthinking amateur radicals and all-too-clear-thinking professional revolutionaries. At least in their thought processes, these millions of middle Americans have left the middle and drifted off into emotional empathy with the Mao Right. Every inane type who demands revolution to "kill the pigs" guarantees recruits to the real fascists and the real pigs.

And when some of those unthinking and soul-sick fools carry names like Rubin, Hoffman, and Rudd, too many Americans forget all the others—the Aryan type gentiles—who joined with these in their madness. All that is remembered is the Jew. How many Jewish graves did the Rubins—who do not even want to be Jewish and who reject their Jewish past and who spit on it and who are the greatest of anti-Semites—dig? They destory themselves and bring down other Jews with them.

And yet, the linking of the Jew with the left is the supreme irony, because it is the Marxist-Leninst dedication to internationalism which makes the Left a deadly enemy of Jewish survival. The Left, bound by a belief in world proletarian internationalism, finds itself the enemy of a separate nationalist Jewish existence. If Lenin decreed that "Marxism cannot be reconciled with nationalism be it even of the most 'just,' 'purest,' most refined and civilized brand"; and if he said that "in place of all forms of nationalism, Marxism advances internationalism," then the Jew, as a separate national entity, must disappear. On the other hand, if Marxism looks upon religion as a dangerous opiate that retains class consciousness, the Jew as a religious unit cannot survive. For the Jew, there is, therefore, only the way of historical oblivion. This, indeed, is what would await the Jew in the event of a Marxist-Leninist victory.

And consider the opposition and violent antipathy to the State of Israel that is led, in the United States, by the Left. The same who call for violent overthrow of the American government, for victory for Hanoi in Vietnam, for uprisings against American "imperialism" throughout the world also support the Arabs in their war on Israel. It is a principle of the radical Left that the State of Israel be eliminated. They support the most extreme of the Arab terrorists and condemn Israel as an aggressor, fascist, racist expansionist state to be lumped into the same pariah class as Rhodesia and South Africa. As the war in Southeast Asia draws to a close, one can expect the Middle East to become the major center of Left preoccupation, with Israel taking the place of Saigon as the major enemy of all "progressive" people and Vietnamese leaders having to make way as the world's chief criminals before Israeli generals. Together with the United States, Israel will be the enemy.

At the same time, attacks upon Israel and upon the Zionist ideology that created and sustains it must inevitably lead to hatred of the Jew, for it is the Jew who supports Israel, and it is the consensus of the vast majority of American Jews that Israel must be supported and defended at all cost. Attacks upon Zionists become, in the end, attacks upon Jews, as witness the Polish, Czech, and Panther charades.

It all goes hand in hand with the outright support given by the Left to the most vicious of anti-Jewish charges at home. In its backing of minority groups who openly speak of specifically *Jewish* landlords or *Jewish* gouging merchants, in their backing of outrageous attacks upon Jews for giving money to Israel that was "stolen" from the ghetto, in echoing the painting of the Jew as the chief enemy of minority groups, the Left aids and abets Jew-hatred. The fact that so many Jewish Leftists shout these obscenities the loudest is not relevant. The worst anti-Semites are the Jewish kind; few Jew-haters can reach the pinnacle of the self-hating Jewish one. Indeed, it is the supreme irony that the Left, which is the deadly enemy of the Jew, should be tied, as an albatross, to his neck so as to destroy him.

The Left brought deadly fear to America and linked the Jew to it. What it, and so many foolish people began, the radical Right will yet finish. The Left prattled about fascist Amerika, and they, together with economic disaster, will yet bring it about.

For on top of our racial, political, and social problems comes the spark that could set off the powder keg upon which we sit. The land of the mighty dollar—the American economic colossus—is suddenly shaken, and the economy is shown to be a paper one.

The sands of time seem to be running out fast in this era of events that fly past us and of time that races by our confused and puzzled brows. Governments speak of huge layoffs and breadwinners are confronted with the unique prospect of unemployment. The welfare state is suddenly incapable of welfaring, and millions who had become accustomed to its omnipotence are suddenly rudely awakened, frightened and angry.

The nation speaks in terms of x number of unemployed, but who is to measure the underemployed and the semi-employed and the millions upon millions who work and cannot live upon wages that are too low to begin with and that are mutilated by an unstoppable inflation? The national average is deceptive, for it does not give proper credit to the ability of major industrial states to have larger unemployment rates and certain key cities to break all sorts of records for idleness.

There are areas that find one man in every six helping his wife tidy up the house because there is no need for him to punch a clock.

The cities stand under a massive cross-country threat of bankruptcy. Indeed, if it were not for some massive, deceitful juggling of figures, many would long since have gone under. Services are shoddy or nonexistent, and the decay is painfully obvious. The sudden economic crisis is heightened by the psychological fact that for twenty-five years we have lived a relatively good life and have come to look upon that beautiful life as that which is our due. We lack the discipline not to be selfish and we do not possess the moral strength to lower our desires. We have come to accept jobs with constantly rising wages as natural, and so our civil servants can ask for astronomical raises in the face of an empty city cupboard. Our bitterness grows in proportion to our rising expectations, just as those expectations rose in proportion to our increasing tastes of the good life.

The masses of blue-collar workers who have gotten used to the luxury of their own private homes and their cars and their paid vacations and their spoiled children and all the affluence that they have tasted in the last quarter century will not, any longer, settle for anything less than this. He who is poor his whole life is not half as dangerous as one who was poor, rose to sip of the good life for a moment, and is now threatened with a reversion to poverty. The former knows not what he is missing: the latter knows it all too well and will, under no circumstances, go back to steerage. It was difficult enough to combat the ravages of inflation that saw him forced to hold two jobs merely to buy that which could be purchased so much cheaper just a few years ago. To compound this with a threat of unemployment is unthinkable. It is unacceptable.

And so, in this year of 1971, as unemployment and fear reach the highest peaks since 1938 and when, for the first time since World War II, many millions of white, blue-collar workers face bleak and painful economic futures, the Jew must once again consider what may be for him. People who are frightened of their economic future are desperate people, and desperate people are dangerous. They will growl at the welfare recipient and snarl at the competitor for their job and look with envy and hate upon those more fortunate than they.

Desperate people are people who hate, and hate-filled people do all manner of insane and horrible things. All the bitterness of their feelings on the Vietnam war and all their antagonism against minorities and racial groups, all their frustrations over the changing social and moral values and all their failures to deal with the young —especially their own, all their personal neuroses and insecurities and all their pent-up rage over a world they dislike and cannot understand, all their impatience with American humiliations overseas and their fear of revolution at home, all these are thrown into the witch's brew from which comes an explosion. That explosion means the destruction of democratic civilization and the substitution of a brutal, tyrannical totalitarianism. America—

that America that has given us its democratic values and opporunities—is in great danger, and the Jew is in the greatest of all perils.

And because there are, indeed, serious problems and threats to the American democratic process and because the totalitarian Left does pose a threat to freedom and democracy, there is opportunity today for the Haters.

There are groups today that, like furtive jackals, creep into the areas of tension, fear, and frustration and grow fat on its terrible fruits. All the elements of totalitarianism are present, and they lie in the hot summer sun waiting to be harvested by the proper demagogues. There are fascist and Nazi-like groups of all kinds to be found in every part of the country. Their common bond is hatred. They hate the black man, the "un-Americans," the Left, and the "destroyers of the Republic." But most of all they hate the Jew. Others may be held in contempt or in fear, but for the Jew there is all this and more. He is also *hated*. In the minds and writings of the Haters, it is the Jew who is responsible for all the problems. He created all the other enemies of the American way of life, and "look at all the Jewish names of Leftists and un-Americans." He is responsible for blacks and subversives and the Left. He is the architect of American defeats in the world. Behind every bad man is the Jew, and he must be eliminated lest America go under.

The radical Right speaks openly of gas chambers and of eliminating the Jew. Groups train with arsenals of light and heavy weapons. Efforts are made to recruit officers from the armed forces and in the state and local police corps. Every day, untiring efforts are made to persuade other Americans to back the cause and to bring it to power. A campaign to sow hysteria and a sense of urgency to "save the Republic" rages. There are tens of such organizations and hundreds of hate publications that reach millions of Americans. Many of these millions believe what they read and hear. All of them begin to think about it, and times of crisis breed a mood of receptiveness which inclines the ear to words which would otherwise be rejected as lunacy. Evil is born among men who are afraid; tyranny is accepted by those who are insecure.

Others will dismiss this with the time-honored Jewish custom of playing the numbers game: There are only a handful of extremists. How many members have they? What can they do? Let us not be paranoid. . . . This is the argument given by too many Jewish leaders and groups. Let us learn not to play this numbers game. A nation need not have a majority of people who are anti-Semites or extremists to be faced with a serious danger. *Few extremist groups have ever seized power as a majority.* The Bolsheviks were an incredibly small part of the Russian people when they took power. Nazi party membership comprised a small minority of the German people and yet it was able to take power legally. The Nazis were able to persuade well over 40 percent of the German people to vote for them.

Extremists do not need vast numbers of people. They seek only a fairly sizeable group, dedicated, disciplined, and ready to work and sacrifice. Then, aided by the proper political, social and economic conditions, helped by the "neutrality" and apathy of the majority, unopposed by potential victims who refuse to recognize the danger—they move to power.

Is fear of anti-Semitism and the growth of a far Right tyranny in the United States so farfetched? Is it really paranoid? The hard core extremist Right, with its adoration of Hitler and its Nazi-like emblems, represents only the tip of an iceberg.

Many otherwise respectable and decent conservative and patriotic groups, most of whose members are genuinely frightened and disturbed by domestic and foreign trends, also harbor within their membership individuals who are extremists and haters of all kinds. These groups are constantly at the mercy of efforts by the extremists to take control of them and their policies. The growth of problems and fears will tend to radicalize former moderates of the decent Right and lead it and them into the extremist camp.

Tens of millions of other Americans who are unaffiliated with any other group receive publications and propaganda from the Haters. The individuals do not officially join extremist groups but they comprise a vast arsenal of potential ammunition for them. Each time that the Haters flood these people with literature, more seeds have been sown. The seeds become food for thought for people who, long before this, were disturbed by events. Someday, given the proper soil, sun, and rain, these seeds could sprout forth into a terrible and awesomely large crop.

Surely the history of extremism and Jew-hatred in the relatively brief period of time since Jews became a meaningful economic, political, and social force in this country holds within it a grave warning for the future.

Should we not remember the Leo Frank case that saw a young Jewish Atlanta resident convicted of murdering a young girl in a trial that was blatantly anti-Semitic and which saw a leading Populist and political leader declare, *"Jewish Libertines take notice"*?

Should we forget Henry Ford and his *Dearborn Independent* which became a cesspool of anti-Semitism and from whose pages came forth a whole series of articles including the "Protocols of the Elders of Zion" and "The International Jew"? Should we forget the fantastic growth of a fascist movement during the 1930s that saw a man like Father Charles E. Coughlin of Detroit whose weekly radio program reached ten million and who acquired countless devoted followers of his Populist and anti-Semitic teachings? Shall we forget the tremendous following of a man like Gerald L. K. Smith and his national directorship for that most charismatic and dangerous threat to American democracy—Senator Huey Long of Louisiana?

Should we forget Long himself who, had he not been assassinated, would surely have been the man on horseback most needed by the nascent fascist forces to mount a truly powerful attack on American democracy? Should we not remember William Dudley Pelley and his Silver Shirt storm troopers? Should we overlook the America First movement and its ability to attract Charles Lindberg and his admiration of totalitarian fascism as the "wave of the future"?

Should we forget the fascists and anti-Semitic hate-mongerers like Lawrence Dennis, the Iron Guard and its leader, James Banahan, Yorkville fuhrer Joe McWilliams, George Christians, and all the other hoodlum and terror types who gained dangerous support during a decade when Americans had no jobs and went hungry?

Above all should we forget that so much public support for these groups came because they were Populists who called for power to the people and attacked the Jews because they "exploited" the people? That Coughlin's movement was known as the Social Justice movement and that Long spoke in working-class terms?

And for those who will—predictably and superficially—ask whether the demise of these groups and their failure to attain power does not prove that the American democracy is a guaranteed defense against them, the answer is obvious. It was not American democracy that curtailed the power and influence of the anti-Semitic Haters in the 1930s. It was not the good sense of the "people" that brought the disastrous social and economic conditions of the Depression to an end. Ironically enough it was another human disaster that ended the disaster of unemployment and discontent that had threatened to bring to America a fascist, Jew-persecuting regime. It was World War II with its need for war materiel and its opening of defense plants and jobs that suddenly took from the Haters their most powerful weapon. It was Pearl Harbor that destroyed fascism in the United States.

What madness! The Jew in America was aided by Hitler. The American Nazi was defeated by his German counterpart.

We must remember this history of recent American times lest we succumb to the pleasant myth of American exception to the general rule of "Hate the Jew." That which was once such a terrible specter and which was ended only by the "fortune" of war, has been prevented from reoccurring only by a spectacular period of economic good fortune. The vast majority of Americans, the children of those who were breadless and jobless and potential followers of the fascists of the '30s, were recipients of the good life for twenty-five years. Such people are not dangerous in an era when their stomachs are filled and their minds empty of fears and worries. Should this change, however, in times when agonizing tensions and personal economic problems loom menacingly, that which once almost occurred can return to plague the Jew.

The Haters understand this very well, far better than do many Jews. As far back as March, 1963, the late head of the American Nazi Party, George Lincoln Rockwell, wrote:

"Our battle is not planned for today when the White man has two cars, a power lawnmower with a little seat for his lardy bottom, bathrooms with hi-fi and all the rest of the easy living of today's white American, but for the inevitable day when our phony, debt-ridden war scare and "foreign aid" economy blows sky-high. . . . When Americans have nothing they have nothing to lose."

The Haters wait, both on the Left and on the Right.

Each believes that he will harvest the crop of the fallen, bitter, disenchanted, frustrated, and desperate. Each waits as Americans, debt-ridden and living on credit that presupposes a regular income that will pay off the installments and allow further borrowing, suddenly see that income dry up. When debts cannot be paid and foreclosures are made, when citizens, with no other way to turn, seek to cash in their savings bonds at a pace that forces the government to refuse to honor them—those are the "glorious" days that the scavengers of human misery await. Those are the days that the Jew will rue and that he must do all in his power to prevent.

The Haters of the Right wait. It is they who are the ultimate threat to the Jew in the United States. And while they wait they sow their seeds. They propagandize through their literature, their speeches, and their recorded telephone calls. Such men are dangerous because, though their thinking may be shallow and lunatic, they nevertheless think a great deal and work ceaselessly at their trade while we enjoy and ignore.

Let us not fear "overreaction." Quite the contrary; the Jewish curse is underreaction as we learned so painfully in Germany. The Jew will, constantly, try to play down danger. He does not want to hear about it, for it is a painful thing. He has great faith in Democracy and in Liberalism, and so he underreacts, and tells himself that things are not quite as bad as they seem. He plays the numbers game. But there is the real danger. To be a little anti-Semitic is no more logical than to be a little bit pregnant. As soon as anti-Semitism rears its ugly head, it must be stopped because it rages and spreads. Timidity, fear, unreasonable "reasonableness," and insane bending-over-backward guarantee further trouble. They persuade the extremist that he can get whatever he desires. The policy of underreaction is one of a domestic Munich, and appeasement is inevitably disastrous. Extremism breeds and multiplies. Under proper conditions it moves from a relatively small group to power with amazing speed. Understand this and know that it must be dealt with *now* while there is yet time, for nothing will avail us should extremism capture power. There is no such thing as a little anti-Semitism or a little hate. Those groups and those politicians who play a numbers game with us by declaring that the extremist groups are small, do us a disservice. They dig the Jewish grave.

And yet, while the night of the long (Right) knives has not descended, there is open and violent anti-Semitism in America and it comes—for the liberals—from a most disconcerting source. The most flagrant and dangerous actual incidents of Jew-hatred in our times have occurred and are occurring at the hands of minority racial, mostly black, militants.

There is something intensely curious about the Jew and his Establishment leaders. Apparently, to them, not all Jew-haters are the same; some are to be treated differently than others. In certain cases, Jewish leadership screams to the heavens about anti-Semitism armed with only a gut reaction, while in others there is no limit to the amount of explaining away and rationalizing of clear cases of Jew-hatred.

And so we come to the problem of evident, clear-cut, and open hatred of Jews on the part of a significant number of blacks. In particular, as is clear to all who know the facts, in the case of the young blacks and especially the young intellectual blacks in the universities, antipathy to and hatred of the Jew is legion. There is hardly to be found a single campus where the black student group does not speak of Jewish "slumlords" and Jewish "gouging merchants" and Israeli-imperialist pigs. There is not a month that goes by that the cry is not heard that the Jew is the greatest enemy of the black man. Tragically, it is not the moderate black group that has the loyalty of the young black, but rather the militant, anti-Jewish Haters and racists.

Jewish organizations' files are filled with samples of Jew-hating leaflets that have been given out in black areas and in schools. The New York City teachers strike brought forth hatred, attacks, and physical assaults on Jews. We were treated to the sight of black teachers—employees of the most liberal city in the nation—charging that Jews were responsible for the "educational castration" of blacks. We found the head of the black teachers group claiming that there was a deliberate attempt by Jews to suppress blacks. We saw a Leftist-liberal radio station sit quietly by while a black teacher read a poem written by one of his young protégés that, had it been emoted by a Southern redneck, would have brought the Jewish Establishment raging like wild lions.

Assaults on Jewish students and youth—as Jews—

are made by cursing black militants. "Jew-stores" are looted and burned, and "Goldberg" is shaken down for money, and our Jewish leadership is incredibly complacent. How slow they were to see the violent anti-Semitism of the New York City school strike, and how little was done about all the events that preceded the strike itself, events that made it clear that Jew-hatred was raging in black areas. How little was and is done and said about Jewish merchants in urban areas who are the targets of arson and looting. How great is the silence as campuses become hotbeds of open anti-Jewish articles and speeches by black radicals. How awesome the inaction when a Jew-hater of the most extreme kind is the moving force behind the administration of a large Northeastern American city. And how much harder these groups fight other Jew-haters!

All sorts of arguments in defense of this unwillingness to act are made, from the simply ridiculous to the sublimely unbelievable. "The attacks are not made on Jews as Jews; things are not as bad as claimed; overreaction will only make things worse; let us understand the background of black hate; let us not be racists."

The last shall be the first, for herein lies a key to Jewish silence on the very real question of black Jew-hatred. The Jewish leadership and many Jews refuse to fight black anti-Semitism with the necessary vigor because they do not wish to be branded as "racists." Suburban Jews who know little of these problems condemn anyone who speaks of black anti-Semitism as being a "racist." What a vulgar corruption of all that is sane and what a racist concept of humanity lies within the perverted liberal refusal to treat all people equally and exactly as they deserve.

To be *liberal* cannot mean that one condescends to other people. All men are equal, but they should be truly equal—for good and for bad. If a man is good, he is surely good regardless of his origins; if he is bad, he should be handled with equality and labeled evil no matter what or who he is. To do less than this, to grant greater tolerance to a black Jew-hater because one pities him or feels for the past sufferings of the black people, is racism of the worst kind and will be met—by the black man himself—with the contempt it deserves. Worse, it will doom the Jew to ever-growing persecution.

If a Jew is kicked in the teeth and, smiling, declares that he understands the reasons and motivations for the "unfortunate" attack, he is either a coward or a condescending racist. He does not respect himself and therefore does not respect the black man who assaulted him, and his refusal to react angrily is, quite rightly, looked upon with suspicion and with the contempt it deserves. No one who does not respect himself can respect anyone else.

If one behaves like a Nazi he should be treated like one, black shirt or black skin. A black man is no worse than anyone else but neither is he better, and all decent and self-respecting men can understand this. The inexplicable, masochistic drive that sends liberal Jews sprawling at the feet of black intellectuals to be berated, insulted, and spat upon can only result in continued assaults and in ever-growing contempt.

Who is really the racist here? Is it the Jew who sees black Jew-hatred and refuses to act because of his "understanding" of the oppression of the Negro, or the Jew who says that he will fight for the rights of all men to be free of oppression, including freedom for the Jew himself to be safe from assaults of whites and blacks alike? And there is something else.

Perhaps so much of the refusal of Jewish groups to vigorously condemn and move against black Jew-hatred lies in the very great difficulty that any man or organization finds in admitting that it was wrong. Jewish organizations and Jewish liberals in the past took upon their shoulders the task of freeing the black. Jews were at the forefront of the civil rights movement, and Jewish groups were found at any time prepared to give money, bodies, and support for the black cause. They did so because it was one of the mythical Principles of the American Jew that Equality and Liberalism would save *him*. They were wrong. The black nationalist movement dislikes the Jew as much as any other white man and probably more so, because it cannot understand why the Jew is helping him and mistakes it for fear and subtle oppression.

Perhaps Jewish organizational refusal to act vigorously on black anti-Semitism lies in the fact that it has been wrong so often. When a major Jewish organization came out only a short time before the Black-Jewish confrontations in New York City with the results of a survey clearly showing that there was no meaningful black hatred of Jews, they were wrong. When an affiliate of that organization voted for preferential treatment for blacks even as against Jews, they were also wrong.

The liberalism of Jewish organizations was born in the hope that it would save the Jew from anti-Semitism. In certain cases, however, it is this liberalism which leads the Jew down the path of inaction that can destroy him. The black anti-Semite will not hesitate to join with a white racist and Hater so long as the common enemy is the Jew, and the white extremist Hater will march with the black he despises in order to bring down the Jew. In time of crisis all sorts of strange bedfellows will be found.

We have become conditioned to thinking of a white backlash in terms of the poorer, lower-class blue-collar whites turning against the blacks. What we do not contemplate is an alliance of these lower classes, white and black, turning against Jews.

The idea is hardly a fantastic one. White ethnics may fear the blacks and may, in the end, turn on them, but the possibility of their first joining together to attack the "haves," and particularly the Jews whom both resent, is a very real one. In a sense this is what the revolutionary Left is attempting to do when it seeks a lower-class alliance of all poor. While the Left may not advocate specific attacks on Jews by this coalition, the result will be the same. On the other hand, the fascist radical Right, despite its contempt and fear of blacks, has in the past already taken their side against Jews and would join with and promote a white-black alliance specifically aimed at the Jewish people.

Again in the words of Nazi Rockwell:

"And in the last two or three years, the Negroes are becoming anti-Semitic by the millions! Even more important, these Jew-wise Negroes are already at the bottom of the economic pile and have little or nothing to lose by fighting the Jews whom they finally begin to realize are exploiting and using them. The Negro anti-Jewish movement is a most deadly and immediate threat to the Jewish manipulators."

What Rockwell could see then, too many Jewish leaders do not yet see today. But the point to understand is the willingness of Rockwell, who looked upon blacks as "savages" and "apes," to sympathize with their plight so long as the target was the Jew. Both communism and fascism appeal, primarily, to the masses, to the little people, to the poor and disinherited. These people join them, not because of idealism, but because of self-interest. If that self-interest means a temporary alliance of the bitterest of enemies against a common threat, they will join together to eliminate that threat and then turn on each other. This is what could very well happen in the case of frustrated and bitter black and white lower classes and the classical scapegoat, the Jew.

Of all the minorities in this land it is the Jew who has been the most successful, who is the most vulnerable, and who is the object of the most envy and hatred. The liberal and radical assumed that the enemy of the Jew was the one on the higher rung of the social and economic ladder and that Jewish survival depended upon an alliance with those below him. As did those Jews who made similar errors in backing the proletarian movements in Europe, we will learn that this is a grave mistake. Jew-haters will be found both above and below the Jew, and those below will probably be more violent and more dangerous. The white establishment hates the Jew but, being wealthy and powerful, is only interested in keeping him out of its neighborhoods, country clubs, and top executive jobs. The desperate and the poor however want what the Jew has already and, having nothing to lose, will do anything to get it. In its belief that Jewish salvation lies in black power, the Jewish Establishment has been seriously in error, and *we* now pay for it. It is difficult, however, to admit a mistake, especially such a grave one. Thus our Jewish leaders continue to be silent and continue to play into the hands of the American establishment which has a stake in that silence and in its own.

One can understand the silence of liberals of the American establishment when it comes to black anti-Semitism. The liberal politician will not risk the loss of black votes and a black power base in his ambitions for higher office; the liberal, wealthy, and entrenched establishment is delighted that black rage is not aimed at its proper target—the establishment itself; the liberal educator lives all day in the hope that militants will not disrupt his institution and is willing to sacrifice the Jew for it.

But the liberal Jewish Establishment still fails to see and still fails to move, and its failure is both a continuation of its blindness and lack of understanding and an inability to admit that it made a mistake. In any event, it is time to elevate equality to its true and proper dimensions. It is time that we not only moved to treat decent blacks like all other decent people but indecent ones in the same way we treat other anti-Semites. Failure to recognize and act upon this problem will see the Jew driven from the urban areas in which he has his economic, political, and social base and driven back to the point where he was decades ago—if not much, much further.

And so the elements for an explosion are at hand, and let no one say that it cannot happen here. All the problems that have festered for years and which have been ignored by politicians who would rather let things lie than tackle unpleasant realities, have now been joined by that which could be the great spark—growing economic distress—and the extremists are abroad in the land ready to pick up the pieces. Perhaps they await only a leader, the man of charisma who will join them together down the terrible road of totalitarianism. I do not know where it will end; I do not know if the bleakness will become more bleak or the trend more sharply defined. I only know that there are people who speak of gas chambers and of Jewish traitors and elimination of the Yid. I only know that millions of desperate people are listening to them with greater acuteness than before. I only know that I have seen the hate-filled faces of some New York City policemen and I have heard their cries: "Hitler didn't get enough of you" and "This way to the gas chambers." I only know that the German was not an aberration and that gas chambers are not a thing indigenously European.

What happened there can happen again, and the seeds of holocaust are already sown. Will they grow into noxious, choking weeds that will strangle America? I do not know. I only know that those who say that it cannot happen are fools or blind or both. I only know that the Haters look upon the Jew as *the* enemy. I only know that the Jew is the first to go in any holocaust and that the economic envy and religious hatred and irrationality of Jew-baiting are here. I only know that twenty-five years after Auschwitz, anti-Semitism is not the shameful thing it was immediately after the Holocaust. I only know that in the great Jewish power center of New York City open Jew-hatred is manifested on campuses at city government-funded agencies, and in publications. I only know that the New York City teachers strike brought forth hatred of the Jew that was so vicious and so blatant that it made the silence of government leaders and their inaction all the more damning.

I only know that once upon a time there was a good land for the Jew that was called Germany. (It is only with the benefit of hindsight and historical ignorance that we are able to look upon Germany as a land where it was inevitable for a holocaust to occur.) The Jew lived in that land quite as well as he does in certain nations today, and perhaps better. A Jew was Foreign Minister in Weimar Germany; there have been no descendants of Abraham to hold office as Secretary of State in Washington. A Jew helped to draft the Weimar Constitution, and Jews owned newspapers and department stores and were doctors and attorneys and Herr Professors and intermarried and assimilated quite as happily and freely as in other lands in our time. It could not happen there—("What is this, Czarist Russia?")—but it did.

And as it began to happen, and as a mad ex-corporal began to rave, Jewish organizations laughed at him and asked: "How many members does he have? How many followers has he?" And when he began to get more followers, Jewish leaders said that he could not possibly win over really large masses of respectable Germans. And when he began to do that, they said that he could not possibly mean the *German* Jews when he attacked the Juden, and that surely he meant the Ost Juden (the eastern Jews of Poland who were quite as despised by their German Jewish brethren for their ostentatious Jewishness).

But in the end, Germans voted for Hitler and used the democratic process to make his the largest party and bring him to legal power. And in the end, the people placed their own self-interest and stomachs before morality and love of their equal Jewish citizens. And in the end Hitler meant, not only the ugly and uncouth eastern Jews, but all—even the Herr Professoren.

For our own sakes, let one thing be clear and let us not attempt to deceive ourselves. People, in the very best of times, do not very much like other people. People, in the very best of times, are jealous and envious and seek to build their own self-esteem by deprecating others. People, in the very best of times, are ethnically self-centered and tend to narrow the circle of truth as much as possible.

And, above all, let us understand that people, in the very best of times, do not like Jews and that people in America, today, do not like Jews. They do not like them because they are too clever or too rigid, too aggressive or too clannish, too grasping or too much interested in supporting Israel. It is not a thing that is logical and one who can understand it had better search his own psychological condition. For ages we have sought to diagnose the condition in the hope of finding a cure and we have failed. In the end, we are left with the resigned words of Rabbi Shimon Bar Yochai: "It is a natural law that Esau hates Jacob . . . ."

The Jew in America is not liked. The place to see and to hear this dislike is not at the hundred-dollar-a-plate banquets given by Jewish organizations to bestow a brotherhood award on a decent non-Jew. Those who dislike Jews, the nonfamous and the unknown, never come into contact with Jewish patricians and leaders. They sit in their bars or in their modest homes and speak about the Jews who are all communists or the Jews who are bringing in the blacks or the Jews who cheat in their stores or the Jews with all the money. It is in these bars and these homes that history is made. This is where the fate of American Jews will be determined.

There is no less hatred of the Jew today than there once was. That which Sammy had counted on has failed. His insecurity is no less today, now that he has gained his suburban home, than the time when he planned for it in the days when he lived in Brownsville. He longs for peace and security and has not yet found it, and so many of his cherished beliefs have proven to be hollow myths.

All the brotherhood programs and all the ecumenical services will be of no avail should the economic and racial dams burst. All the myths and principles of the American Jew will prove to be paper hopes on that day. In the end it is not Liberalism or Equality or Democracy or Love that moves the non-Jew. It is self-interest. It is time for the Jew to learn this for himself, if he wishes to survive.

But it is not only the failure to eradicate Jew-hatred that the American Jew faces today. After decades of building the new American Jewish life style yet another major disaster has emerged.

THE ALIENATION OF JEWISH YOUTH

Having gained the American socio-economic paradise the Jew proceeded to lose his child. Onward and upward he had climbed in his quest for the Material Nirvana. With every difficult step, he had jettisoned more of his Jewish baggage, the better to be freer and lighter for the drive to the peak. And finally, having overcome the obstacles, having scaled each and every rocky boulder, he looked about for his child and heir and found him missing. Multiply the scene by its thousands and hundreds of thousands and the stark picture of assimilation and alienation, the most dangerous threat to the survival of the Jew as a separate entity, comes into focus. What hath the American Jew wrought!

He looked at the little one his wife had carried and could not recognize him; he called his name and the youth walked away. All that for which Sammy had run and struggled and sweated and labored, his child turned his back upon. The home, the priorities, the good life and more, all rejected. And worse. Sammy had compromised his Judaism and played games with his Jewishness but never had meant for his son to drop it completely. To give up the "superstition" and the outmoded concepts and the things that made it difficult to mix, that was understandable. But, Sammy's child had gone further.

Where the father had merely cheated in his Jewishness, desiring to be Jewish but not *too* Jewish, his son had proceeded not to cheat—*he* dropped it all. Sammy's son simply does not particularly care about being Jewish and sees no disaster in assimilation. And the wailing of puzzled parents desperately trying to understand their children fills the studies of rabbis from coast to coast: "He wants to marry a Mary. I gave him everything; where did I go wrong? True, I wanted him to Melt, but not to dissolve."

Worried, confused, and heartsick, the American Jewish parents sit trying to understand but unable to. Why is it that their child refuses to go to the synagogue services they frequent so faithfully three times a year and shows nothing but contempt for the Temple's Las Vegas nights? Worse, Jewish horror of horrors, how can he break his mother's heart by bringing home a shiksa and then angrily proclaiming that his gentile's home will be no less kosher than the nonkosher Jewish one in which he was raised and that is run by his mother, a good daughter of Sarah? And who can forget his making it quite clear that candles would not be lit in his home on

Friday nights and the chill that shot through his father who feared that, by the same token, he would also neglect to light a yahrtzeit lamp for him, in days to come.

Jewishness leaves their child apathetic—and worse. Not only does he see nothing wrong in intermarriage and in assimilation, but he fails to contribute as he should to the American holy of holies—the United Jewish Appeal. Not only is he not emotionally involved with Israel but he marches, instead, for all sorts of strange causes named Vietnam and Laos and Angola and Mozambique. Indeed, if the truth be known, he sometimes walks around his home and campus allowing that El Fatah and other such cutthroats and Jew-haters are a proper national liberation group. Surely, their child has gone mad.

The number of Jews who have lost their children, in this manner, is staggering. The tragedy is not merely that they, the parents, cannot find their offspring but that a generation is being lost to the Jewish people.

If there were no anti-Semites and if hatred of the Jew could, miraculously, be deported from all the western lands there would still be a disaster confronting the Jew; he would still face annihilation. The Talmud speaks of all various manner of deaths, some painful and some subtly soft. Assimilation is the subtly soft disease that is raging throughout the American and western Jewish body and which threatens it with oblivion.

That which the Church could not do and which the Cossacks could not achieve and that in which Auschwitz failed is being accomplished by the sweet smell of assimilation. There is no greater problem facing the Jew, today.

Conquering it, he survives; succumbing to it means disaster.

The American Jewish child was given the life that his father did not have. He took it, examined it, and threw out whatever Jewishness that remained therein. He is no longer particularly proud of being a Jew, and wave upon wave his peers roll by their parents, devoid of Jewish self-respect and utterly lacking in knowledge of or pride in Jewish people, heritage, past or future.

His parents are troubled to the depths of their souls. In place of pride there is apathy and self-hatred, and instead of Jewish values and priorities they see only a rejection of heritage and a desperate search for other values and goals. On the one hand they find him despairing and turning inward, seeking escape from reality through the drug culture. On the other, they see him reaching for strange causes and stranger gods, many of them non-Jewish and, some, too often, anti-Jewish.

His elders watch in undisguised horror and puzzlement as he rejects all that is holy and revered to them. As he smokes marijuana or, increasingly, shoots heroin into his veins they attempt to comprehend his despair. As he marches with the Left under the banners of El Fatah against the State of Israel they give up in total failure. They do not understand his indifference to Jewry. They fail to comprehend his search for other values. They do not understand him. But we do.

If Jewish campus heroes are black militants and revolutionary guerrillas, the reasons are not beyond comprehension. One who knows nothing of his history and of his own heroes will search out other histories and other heroes because deep within each of us is a compulsive need to admire someone or something and to sacrifice and glorify some ideal.

These Jewish youth who drink, so eagerly, from strange wells are desperately desirous of finding themselves and their own identity. Those who reject Jewishness, secretly yearn for a reason to embrace it. Those who proclaim themselves to be men of the *Internationale* hurt so very much in their longing for personal-and-Jewish identity. The way back for them is a sorely overdue purging of our own souls and a long-needed confession of our own sins.

We understand. We understand all too well what made the alienated Jewish youth the tortured creature that he is. The problem is not that he is the grandchild of a stubborn zeyde but the child of an empty and fraudulent parent.

He has no Jewish pride; can we really blame him? He rejects the glories of Jewishness; is it really his fault? He seeks strange causes because he has none that are Jewish. Is that really so incomprehensible!

It is time that our Jewish adults, leaders, and organizations left their offices where they write about and discuss youth and got out into the schools and the streets where they can meet him face to face and understand him.

To see the solution one must understand the problem and be willing to admit fault. If young Jews today are apathetic and indifferent to Jewishness; if they march for non-Jewish and, sometimes, anti-Jewish causes, the fault lies not in their stars but in ourselves.

If it upsets us that Jewish heroes on campus are named Fidel and Che and Ho, or that Jewish causes are aimed at freeing anti-Jewish black militants, shall we not ask ourselves whether we ever taught them the names of Dov Gruner or Ben Yosef or Hakim? To be more embarrassingly persistent, do we know the names ourselves?

In an era when young Jews recognize the names and the legitimacy of all foreign national liberation movements they remain steadfastly ignorant of the fact that a Jewish freedom movement in our times even existed. The Vietcong is known and the Pathet Lao and the NLF, but the names of the Irgun and the Lechi (Sternists) and Hagana remain mysteries. Black and Puerto Rican and yellow and Asian martyrs are common knowledge. Gruner, Irgun Zvai Leumi member, who was hanged by the British following an attack upon a colonialist police station, or Ben Yosef, who was the first Jewish nationalist to go to the gallows in Palestine, or Hakim, who struck down a British official who turned back immigrant ships, remain dark secrets.

And is it strange? Where did they hear these names at home or in school or in synagogue? Where did the vitally needed Jewish pride in liberation movements come to the young Jewish boy or girl whose only knowledge of modern Jewish history consisted of six million Jews going to their death like lambs? They never knew of the pride of Jewish resistance in Palestine or the glory of Jewish partisan groups in Eastern Europe. They only know of Jewish sacrifice. They need pride, they need self-assurance, they need knowledge of their bravery and strength. They never received it.

Those who were never given Jewish pride can never possess it. Those who were never given meaningful Jewishness cannot take pride in it. Those who were never given an insight into their grandfather's stubborn obsession cannot share in it. Those whose lack of knowledge of things which would give them pride in self and people, will search out other causes and other peoples, will carry within themselves masochism and hatred of self, parents, religion, rabbis, synagogue, and nation.

The alienated young Jew is the product of an empty and vapid culture, a neo-Jewishness of gold and silver. What sensitive man cannot help but share his disgust? He was given dross and told it was Judaism; tinsel and told it was Jewishness. Little wonder that he was repelled, that he rejected it out of hand. He was defrauded and robbed of his true birthright by parents, temples and Establishment. He was never given true Judaism or Jewishness. Therein lies the tragedy and—paradoxically —the hope. For if one understands that what he was offered was not his birthright, perhaps he will yet go back and inspect the real thing. But, for that, he must be convinced.

Let us look at the American Jewish youth of our time. Born in a home one step away from the Judaism of centuries, of a family, one or two generations removed from the ghetto and poverty. At great cost and with mighty effort his parents or grandparents escaped from their economic bondage and from the Great Depression.

They made their money during the war or perhaps they had already found their fortune and moved from the old areas. How great was the Exodus! From the all-Jewish neighborhoods of Brownsville and East New York and Flatbush and the Bronx (one can fill in the names of every other urban Jewish area) the Jews moved to the suburbs. A gentile may buy a house for a home but Jewish parents do it as an investment or as a temporary residence until they can move a little further up the ladder of social and economic status.

The father worked and the mother planned and the house was the center of social aspirations. The snobbery grew with the length and number of autos. The winter of Jewish discontent had passed and the voice of materialism was heard in the land. The Jew was now on Long Island and Westchester, in a frantic race to emulate and integrate with the gentile. And so he learned to drink and get drunk—O Western man! And so he gambled on the horses and lowered his sideburns and joined the others in the endless race for fun, fun, fun. He elevated Miami Beach to breathless heights, and the Catskills became a unique Jewish cesspool of material ostentatiousness.

The old Orthodox synagogue was simply unthinkable in the new areas and Reform and Conservatism flourished, the former so that the Christian neighbor might favorably be impressed and the latter because many Jews were not quite courageous enough to go that far in one fell swoop. Ideology never entered into these changes. Jews switched because their wives did not like to be separated from them during services or because the rabbi did not frown on driving to temple on the Sabbath.

The key word here was "convenience." The Jew who was now able to buy everything was also now able to acquire a custom-made religion. Fraudulent? Of course, but a garment-center man or Wall Street plunger learned to accept this without blinking an eye.

"Where did we go wrong?" One can begin right here. The Judaism that we left behind in Brooklyn and which was traded in for a newer sleek, convenient model is as good a place as any to begin to find where the American Jew went wrong. It was here in the suburbs and here in his sleek temple where he perpetrated the fraud on himself and on his child.

One of the most incisive and moving analyses of "where they went wrong" was given by a young Jewish City College of New York student named Jonathan Braun. Himself a peer of the Jewish child who chose to dissolve and who broke his Jewish parents' hearts, himself of the generation of Jews who chose to drop their Jewishness rather than play games with it, Braun writes:

> The Assimilationists went "wrong" when they ceased being Jews and became, instead, Americans of the Jewish faith. They went "wrong" when they replaced the Sabbath meal with the TV dinner, the

chalah with the package of cheese doodles, the synagogue with the bowling alley, in short, when they deserted a rich and beautiful culture of two-thousand years for a cult of plastic pizza-eaters who retain their Judaism by peppering their conversation with a few Yiddish expressions and frequent comments on the superiority of Jewish rye bread. . . .

And their children, the products of a protestantized, Borscht-Belt Judaism (a hollow model based on the interpretations of Jewish law by wedding and bar mitzvah caterers) raise clenched fists before the popposter ghost of Che Guevara.

The children of the Establishment Assimilationist have left Miami and Queens Boulevard to build communes in the American wilderness, publish nihilist newspapers in the East Village, cut sugar cane in Cuba, and, in some extreme cases, run obstacle courses in Arab terrorist training camps.

And the parents, the well-meaning, middle class parents who so terribly wanted their Cathy and Eric to be 100% Americans, are puzzled. Why, they ask, are their children dressing like Gypsies, wearing Afros, and smoking dope?

"Where did I go wrong?"

It began with the fraud that Jewish parents perpetrated on themselves. It ended—disastrously—when they attempted to foist that fraud on their child.

Having built for themselves their convenient kind of Judaism it was important that their child be exposed to the culture of his people. One should carefully note that it was not so much religion or nationalism that was at stake here, but "culture." Religion is for rabbis and nationalism for Panthers. For the American Jew "culture" had the proper ring to it. Off went the grandson of an outmoded zeyde to learn Jewish culture. Off went Scott, the son of Abraham, to partake of his Judaism.

They tell a story about a young Jewish rabbi who acquired his first pulpit. As he rose to begin his sermon that first Sabbath the president advised him not to preach about the Sabbath or kashrut or other prohibitions. When the rabbi asked him what he should talk about, the president looked at him in surprise and replied: "Why Judaism, rabbi, talk about Judaism."

The Judaism of Scott's parents, the Jewish culture to which they wished him exposed, consisted primarily of two things: Making sure their son came home with a Shirley instead of a Mary and seeing to it that their offspring would be properly sacrificed to the great American Jewish god, the caterer, in that unique temple rite known as the Bar Mitzvah.

Let us hear the conclusion of the whole matter: Study the Word and enter the Bar Mitzvah rite, for this is the whole duty of American Jewish man.

Jewish education is a sometime thing in the U.S. The Jewish child is taken by the hand at the age of ten or eleven and enrolled in what we euphemistically call a Hebrew school. Is he brought there to become an observant or learned Jew? Hardly. One cannot be expected to continue the outmoded and inconvenient rituals of kashrut and the burdensome Sabbath. The three-times-a-week trek of Scott is for loftier purposes. He sits in the labyrinth of Hebrew hieroglyphics so as to make, in two or three years, some caterer happy and his father debt-ridden. It is the Bar Mitzvah that drives his parents to educate him; it is the Bar Mitzvah that will end his thirst for Jewish knowledge. It is the mother's drive for status and glitter, the parents' insane, competitive race to bankruptcy that will ruin the father financially and the son spiritually.

The new American Jewish temple; the new American Jewish religion of convenience; the new American Jewish education of Scott, son of Abraham; the Bar Mitzvah. All part of the American Jewish way of death, and the young Jew is its primary victim: The Jewish business-industrial complex destroyed every vestige of meaningfulness and sacrificed him to its monstrosity. Off he went to Hebrew School to acquire Jewish "culture."

And there, occasionally, he gleaned some drops of true Jewish wisdom and tradition. The occasional Jew occasionally learns something substantive. His rabbi tells him of strange and interesting things, such as kashrut. He informs him that Jews do not eat bacon—startling news to one who that very day . . .

But children are capable of sacrifice and the world is rather black and white when you are ten years old. And the Jewish child, filled with faith in the omniscience of his rabbi, comes home to inform his parents of the

Truth. Bacon, he announces, is from that moment on, verboten; orders of the Almighty.

He is speedily disabused of such naiveté. That absurdity is quickly disposed of. "We are not sending you there for *that, Scott.*"

The young Jew listens and understands—all too well. He understands because one cannot deceive children; they are too perceptive and too understanding. He understands that it is not for Judaism that he is being sent to his Temple, the repository of Judaism, but to set new records for skyrocketing expenses and obscene ostentatiousness. He perceives that it is all a sham and understands that it is full of sound and fury, signifying nothing. The dishonesty and hypocrisy grate upon his sensitive soul and, though he continues to play the game— when it is finally over, it is *all* over. Today, young Jew, you are a man; disillusioned, cynical, and searching. The young Jew was told not to take his Judaism seriously. He does not. He gives it up entirely.

His Judaism, for most practical purposes at an end, the young Jew goes out into the world to find his own values and to choose his own road in this improbable world. There is one who becomes apathetic, not only to Jewishness but to every other ideal. Life, for him, becomes a series of socio-economic rungs on a ladder. The more rungs one climbs the higher one gets and the clearer it becomes that there are more rungs than most people think.

Such a one becomes, despite himself, his father's son and molded in his image. His Jewishness is paler, but the great apathy allows for no great emotion either for or against the Jewishness that he left. He is prepared, if so it works out, to marry a gentile; he will not support Israel quite as strongly as his father; there will be little semblance of anything Jewish left, but he will follow his father's social life style.

There is yet another who becomes more Catholic than the Pope and who outdoes his elders in supping at the fleshpots. He leaps into the ocean and drinks deeply of the good life, luxuriating in the sweetness of its smell. He takes what his parents gave and multiplies it a hundred-fold, and his occasional protests against "materialism" even as he luxuriates in it, evoke little sympathy. His road to decadence is one that climbed from the luxury of the good life to that of the sinful and onwards and upwards to the illegal and the perverted and the irrational. He who has everything except true values is a thirsty man who quenches himself with ocean water. The salt drives him on to yearn for all that man can possibly conceive and much that he cannot. He lives for himself, and the love affair is truly epic.

And then, there is the one who moves on in a different direction. His yearning is not to escalate the vapidness of his parents—but a desperate effort to find something that is qualitatively different. Substance, oh substance, where art thou substance!

Perceptive and analytical, he tasted life in the affluent, gilded ghettos and found it wanting. He may not have accepted much else from his Torah but he understood the words, "not by bread alone shall man live." And to it, he added, from a wealth of experience, nor "even by cake." Unable to find himself and a meaning to his life, he thrashed about desperately, a Jewish Diogenes searching everywhere for an honest answer to what it was all about. The search led in two directions.

When there is no pride in self-identity or roots in people and heritage there cannot be self-respect. There remains only self-contempt and hatred. The self-hate, this feeling of hopelessness and rootlessness, inevitably leads to a desire for self-destruction and gives rise to the death wish. At times this remains within the individual and leads to his own personal destruction. At other times it leads to the concept: "Let my soul die with the Philistines," and the self-hating individual becomes wrapped up in mindless and heedless anarchy, wishing to take as many others as possible with him in his flight to self-destruction. In the one case the whole bag of boredom, emptiness, vapid existence, and aimless social climbing is shut off with drugs, and the young Jew joins new congregations. He turns inward, seeking escape and self-destruction through narcotics, hedonism, or suicide.

There are others who seek their self-destruction by joining the maddest of revolutionary groups and the most irrational of terrorist bombers. They will go under and take as many as possible with them.

And there are those who sense a more rational approach. They have no desire to seize upon a drug culture that clearly is a hell in which they do not seek to acquire permanent residence. Nor do they seek to end their lives in irrational, mad adventure. They seek a cause—any true cause—that will turn them on. Descendants of a people of the cause, needing an ideal as plants need the sun and the rain, thousands of young Jews search desperately, plough anxiously in strange vineyards, seeking Truth.

They thought they found what they wanted in the universities where revolution beckoned to them and where causes were thrown into their laps. The extremists understood full well the key to the young Jew. Never seek to give something—rather demand idealism and sacrifice from him. This is the language that the young Jew understands; this is the water for his parched soul.

In his family he was given nothing—he found it elsewhere. His schools and synagogues failed to give him Jewish heroes—he found his ideals in things un-Jewish. "Why have I called and no one answers?" The words of Isaiah echo and ring forth from ancient times. They echo once again in our times, but the voice is that of our youth.

The death of Jewishness in America began with the desperate fear of anti-Jewishness. In our terrible obsession over preservation of our bodies we dismantled our souls and spirit. In the end, we will have lost not only our youth and spiritual future but we will not even be able to save our bodies. The time has come for a long hard look; the time has come for an accounting of our souls.

For it is not only our youth that has lost its identity and gropes in the darkness of spiritual amnesia for some light unto its name, it is the Jewish father and mother, too. It is the adult American Jew who built the spiritual mausoleums and who gilded his ghetto and who knows, too well, that he has lost something pricelessly meaningful somewhere along his climb to the mortgaged castle in the suburbs. His home is a paper haven, for it is filled with possessions, not respect and love. If the definition of a wealthy man is one who is satisfied with his lot, then the American Jew knows that he is on spiritual welfare.

Something basic is gone out of the life of the Jew, young and old. He has lost the thread of his past, is fearful of the unknown future, and does not know what the present means. He is a flower plucked from its roots and cast away, a ship cast from its moorings and in danger of being swamped by massive waves. He does not really know what he is or, more important, *why* he is.

Our Jewish youth looks at the black minority and secretly envies its concept of "soul." He listens to talk of "brothers and sisters" and is jealous. They, so poor and so disadvantaged, apparently have what he has not. He longs for self-respect and pride in self. And that is where the resurrection of the Jew begins.

It is not true that there is no hope for the Jew and that the spark of identity, pride, and self-respect are beyond him. It is not true that the young Jew is dead to his people and that we must begin to say the kaddish over him.

I have seen the resurrection of the young Jew. I

have seen his eagerness to be Jewish and his drinking thirstily from the fountain of Jewishness. I have seen his face light up and his soul glow, and I have seen him grasp his Jewishness by the hand and walk proudly with it as with his sweetest lover.

I have seen thousands of young Jews go to the capital of the United States and sit in her streets to be arrested for Soviet Jewry. I have sat with those young Jews and watched as they were led away to jail to make world headlines, shouting—of all things—"Never Again" and "Am Yisroel Chai" (the people of Israel live). Wonder of Wonders, and Blessed Be the L-rd! Here were Jews marching and being arrested, not for Southeast Asia or Mozambique or Antartica, but for Jews. Here were Jews defying all the laws of the 1960s and crying out for their own people.

He who was not there and he who was not privileged to see the sight of young Jews, with faces shining and eyes sparkling, walking to the police vans and crying, "Bring more buses," has never known real Jewish nachas. Are our children really lost to their people, you ask, as you behold the huge Hillel buildings naked in their emptiness? Can we ever win back the lost Jewish flocks, you inquire as you behold the huge Temple budgets for youth programs and the minuscule results they produce? Have no fear; there is hope, magnificent hope.

When thousands can come to Washington and hundreds upon hundreds demand arrest; when row after row of proud young Jews—some with yarmulkas, some with long shaggy hair—march together for their people five thousand miles away; when long lines of young Jews—some religious, some totally removed from religion—can stride together and cry: "We are Jews, we couldn't be prouder, and if you can't hear us, we'll shout louder"; when the strange and foreign causes are laid aside and it is Leningrad and Riga that pull our young people—there is hope.

But as you beam with pride and as you savor its flavor remember how this miracle came about and think carefully into this resurrection of our youth.

It was not speeches and programs that won them back and not sermons and YMHA basketball leagues. It was not the huge and ornate temples or the Jewish hospitals funded by the Federations. It was not the pap that is given them in the after-school-hour religious schools or the interfaith services at the local synagogue. It was nothing that we gave them; rather it was what we took from them.

If you want to win back Jewish youth, do not offer them things—demand this of them. Demand *sacrifice* —real sacrifice. Insist upon idealism—true idealism. Take from them their souls and their spirit and they will follow. Show them the way up the mountain, but walk there first—before them—and they will climb with you to the heights of danger.

Those who sit in their executive suites can never win Jewish youth and those who limit their Jewish crusades to press releases will never see such faces as we saw that week. Above all, those who decry hooliganism and those who rail against militancy speak foreign tongues to the young Jew.

It is not militancy that disturbs him; it is rather the long years that he waited for someone to demand it of him. It is not the lack of respectability that drives him away, but rather the decades of stultifying "nice Irvingism." Suddenly he has seen something new, something that captures him and carries him up in Jewish intensity. Suddenly people have stopped telling him that Jews must bleed for the world and shout out to him: Jewish is beautiful.

He likes what he hears, and the terms "Jewish hooligan" and "militant" have a sweet ring to them. He wonders what might have been had there been more such ones around thirty years ago.

I repeat. The young Jew—and the adult, too—longs for self-respect and pride in self. And that is where the resurrection of the Jew begins.

JEWISH PRIDE

One of the great Jewish leaders of our time, or indeed of many other Jewish eras, was the legendary Zev Jabotinsky: creator of the Jewish Legion, first Jewish fighting force since Roman days; founder of the Hagana during the first modern Arab anti-Jewish riots in Jerusalem; spiritual father of the Jewish revolutionary fighting forces Irgun and FFI (Sternists); visionary of a Jewish state when others shrank from the concept. Jabotinsky carved out his achievements from a philosophy he called by its Hebrew name, Hadar.

Hadar means pride; Hadar means dignity; Hadar means self-respect. Jabotinsky roamed Eastern Europe in the days between the two great wars and spoke to Jews suffering from physical Jew-hatred and from the mental inferiority of centuries of persecution; Jews who had come to accept the pogram as something natural.

The sun rises and the sun sets and the pogrom comes and it goes—this was the resigned philosophy of a people whose backs were bent and whose heads were bowed by two millennia of unparalleled degradation and persecution.

Jabotinsky spoke to these Jews, whom he loved so deeply and for whom his very being wept. Listen Jews, he said, there is no mitzvah (Jewish commandment) that decrees that a Jew must be beaten like a dog. There is no obligation to die like cowering sheep. Stand tall, he cried out, stand with pride and with dignity and give back as much and more than you get.

Wherever he would come, the crowds of ghetto and shtetl Jews would come to hear and their eyes would light up as their backs straightened listening to the words of Hadar that Jabotinsky had written and which he echoed forth in majesty:

> Hadar! A Jew, even in poverty, is a prince.
> Whether servant or serf you were created the son of kings,
> Crowned with the diadem of David;
> In light or in darkness, remember the crown . . .

Hadar begins with a proclamation of a Jew's own self-worth and dignity. It means stating to all who would hear—or not hear—that the Jew may not be better, in their eyes, than others—but he will not be taken for worse. It means an affirmation of self-respect and a demand for respect from others. It means the burial of our neurotic need to be loved.

We Jews are obsessed with love. By this I mean the

compulsive need to have the world, the non-Jew, love us. It is a product of the centuries of Galut—exile—in which sufferings, persecutions, and holocausts engendered within us fears, insecurities, and inferiority complexes of all kinds. No matter how loudly we proclaim our equality, no matter belligerently we insist that we are really accepted, deep in our hearts we are not sure; we desperately need reassurance.

And so we attempt to buy the love of the non-Jew in a hundred and a thousand different ways. If he frowns on the Jewish ethical standards that separate us from the madding crowd we are only too eager to accomodate him by accepting lower and more animal virtues. We show that we can drink and carouse with the best of people and that our divorce rate can be as high as all the rest. We suspect that he finds our traditional forms of worship and observance unacceptable and so we modify them for his convenience so that we might find favor in his eyes. How eagerly we yearn for ecumenism so that we might show our neighbors that we are truly civilized and so that we might have an opportunity to bask in the glory of a minister or priest deigning to grace our pulpit. Indeed the glory of our Temples Emanuel lies in their ability to look and feel like churches.

We attempt to buy love, too, by marching for all causes in the world and by sacrificing for any and all peoples. We march for Vietnam—perhaps they will love us then—and demonstrate for all the world—perhaps they will embrace and accept us in every wretched corner. Rabbis will get arrested for civil rights in Alabama, and Jewish organizations will explain away black racism and anti-Semitism, and Jewish leaders will admit responsibility for crimes committed long before there was a Jewish presence. Our Jewish Federations will find all means of non-Jewish causes and pour Jewish money into every people while our own needs go begging. All in the hope that we might buy love and feel securer in a world that, quite rightly, we suspect still hates us.

What we have not yet learned, even after the Holocaust that swept through Europe from a land in which Jewish roots extended back a thousand years and which saw the Jew convinced of his acceptance and equality, is that the possibility of the Jew ever winning the world's love is dubious and that, in any event, before one can even hope to win love he must first gain respect.

But one does not gain respect by asking for it or by buying it. One gains respect by earning it, and it begins with self-respect. For the gentile understands full well, far better than the desperate Jew, that the man who cannot respect himself is never capable of respecting anyone else. If one is a self-hater, he surely harbors contempt for everyone else, and his pious proclamations of love are merely shallow efforts at using people for his own ends.

Behind our pious proclamations of tolerance of anti-Semitism lies the fear of fighting back. Back of our willingness to shamefully absorb contemptuous slurs is our effort to prove to ourselves that they are not really indicative of general thinking and that really we are accepted and loved. In reality, however, we know the bitter truth, and the gentile, who watches with amazement at Jewish willingness to be kicked and slandered without protest, adds even more contempt to his image of the Jew.

Thus, a particular, noted television personality— Jewish, by birth—invites a racist and anti-Semite on his television show. The latter, whose fame has come from such weighty comments as: "We don't want any more Goldbergs, Weinsteins, or boobies," begins by insisting that he will refer to the commentator as "pig." The latter smiles through the inquisition, thus reinforcing in the mind of every normal watcher the image of the Jew as a "patsy," as one who is capable of being pushed around, as one so lacking in self-respect as to be less than a man.

Thus, a leading offical of a Jewish Establishment group appears on a nationally syndicated television program along with a vicious anti-Semite whose article concerning planned Jewish efforts to "educationally castrate" black children aroused a furor. The Jewish official tells him that he owes him an apology of sorts for not having met with him *before* condemning him since he has now found him to be a reasonable man. Impossible? Would that it were so . . . .

An extremist demands reparations from Jews for the sins committed by Baptist slave owners. Rest assured that there are Jews to be found who are only too eager to confess their guilt. A leading Reform rabbi beats his breast as he has not done for forty years on Yom Kippur and avows his guilt for all the sins committed by the ancestors of the non-Jewish American establishment.

Now it may be that this particular rabbi did, indeed, have Baptist ancestors, but most Jews do not, and most of them came here in steerage, poverty stricken and fearful, fleeing from a Europe that oppressed them in at least as many ways as the blacks were oppressed here. They owe nothing, and that is precisely the amount of reparations that should be paid.

And so, when a group of Jews—outraged and indignant—stand up against this crude blackmail by coming to a prestigious temple which has been the target of the extortion and declare that no precedent of surrender shall be set here, they are met with outrageous protests by the fearful Jews.

In a veritable flood of indignation Jewish organizations and leaders condemn Jews who dared to stand with bats and pipes and thus convinced the blackmailer not to pollute a synagogue with his presence. How does one explain to these Jews that respectability must be buried before it buries us? How does one make them comprehend that the image of the Jew as a lemming, whether in this instance or in all the other cases of assaults upon Jewish rights, must be changed in the only language that the hoodlum and bully understands? How does one proclaim that, if such things are permissible to all others, the Jew cannot be asked to be more Catholic than the Pope?

Hadar means a reaffiirmation and rephrasing of the Golden Rule: "That which you would not want done unto yourself, you had better not do to the Jew."

We are told by the rabbis that when the Almighty wanted to give the Torah to the Jewish people, instead of choosing some lofty and majestic mountain, he selected a small, humble little mound, barely more than a hill, named Sinai. His purpose, it is explained, was to show that man must turn his back on overbearing pride and false ego. The Jew must be humble.

It is related that, when the Gerrer Rebbe (one of the great Hassidic scholars of the last hundred years) studied this particular portion of the Talmud, he paused and commented: The Almighty's intentions were, indeed, laudable. Nevertheless, he could have done better. If he intended to teach the Jew not to be a mountain and to be humble, why was the Torah not given in a valley? Surely there is nothing more humble than a valley . . . .

The answer that he gave was clear and bold. The Almighty, he said, wanted to teach us a second lesson; one that was quite as important as the first. It is not enough to merely reject pride. Too much humbleness is, itself, wrong. A Jew must have pride; a Jew must not allow himself to be stepped on like a valley. Otherwise, he is not a Jew—or a man.

The great oaks of Auschwitz grow from little acorns of fearful backing away from a confrontation. Failure to have self-pride, and fear of refusing to be stepped upon, as if a valley, always results in continued, and worse, assaults. For too long, there has been an unofficial Jewish Association of Masochists based upon stringent entrance requirements which call for an ability to be berated and insulted while smiling; beaten and kicked while shouting happily, "Beat me again!"; whipped, villified, and threatened while denying that there is any problem; and hours of intensive breast-beating.

Jews of that stripe are the ones who set up tables at local high school and college campuses to raise money for a militant so that he might better continue his attacks on "Zionist pigs." Wealthier ones, of course, throw cocktail parties and invite all their chic friends. (For the rich Jew who has everything what do you buy?—a Panther.) Jews of that association make speeches from the pulpits admitting Jewish complicity in the oppression of minorities here and seeing nothing wrong in reverse discrimination that effectively bars qualified Jews from schools and employment. Jews such as that devote their lives for all other cause but give little or nothing for their own people.

Other people, when hit, strike back. It is only this ghetto-minded Jew who, when struck, will intellectualize and consider: Perhaps, I deserved it.

But aside from such to-be-pitied Jews, there are the all-too-many who deplore attacks upon Jews but who counsel us "not to make waves" and who convinced us that Jewish reaction "only makes things worse." It is this unwillingness to take a small, unpleasant step while there is still time that guarantees we will be forced, in time to come, to attempt much worse in our own defense. And by that time it may be too late.

Backing away from a confrontation is, generally, the surest way of guaranteeing it. The image of the Jew as an easy mark, as one who backs off, as one who allows himself to be pushed back, as a "patsy," is the image that must be changed.

Only when the Jew has the respect of self and only when he declares that he stands first and foremost for Jewish rights and self-interest will anyone really believe him when he maintains that he respects the rights of others. Only when he fights for himself can he really fight for anyone else.

And if Jewish liberals who have thrown so much of themselves and their efforts into the battle for civil rights, only to be rejected, are puzzled at their treatment at the hands of those for whom they struggled, let them understand now. The Jewish liberal, who turned his back on his own cause and claimed that he loved and fought for others, was a patent fraud and was recognized as such by all—especially by those whom he was helping. No man can love another if he does not love himself and no man who cares nothing for his own liberation is to be believed when he claims to want to liberate others. One cannot run from himself; one cannot hope to escape his Jewishness. In the end, the non-Jew will not allow it. In the final analysis the gentile insists that the Jew remain a Jew.

The Galut image of the Jew as a weakling, as one who is easily stepped upon and who does not fight back, is an image that must be changed. Not only does that image cause immediate harm to Jews but it is a self-perpetuating thing. Because a Jew runs away and because a Jew allows himself to be stepped upon, he guarantees that another Jew in the future will be attacked because of the image which he has perpetuated. Furthermore, in running away the Jew comes to believe that he is indeed weak, that he is indeed a coward. He, himself, begins to lose the last shred of his confidence and his self-respect. He guarantees that the next time, he will run away again —and the time after that and after that. So much of the self-hate that we find among our Jewish youth arises from their contempt for what they consider to be their own and the general Jewish weakness.

It is not enough to merely speak of Jewish suffering and holocaust. Indeed, to continually emphasize the slaughter of Jews adds to the image of the Jew as a weak, defenseless being, adds to the contempt that the Jew has for himself and his people and creates the self-hatred that is the phenomenon of too many Jews today.

Jewish rights must not be allowed to be trampled on, for if the hoodlum and anti-Semite is allowed a small victory his greed will grow and we will be assured of further and greater problems. Jewish suffering does not go away because we ignore it. To the contrary, it increases. If a Jewish right is trampled, there must be an immediate response, strong but responsible, militant but carefully thought out, soft words but determined position. No anti-Semite was ever created because Jews stood up for what was rightfully theirs, and no anti-Semite ever came to repent because Jews allowed him to take from them their rights.

Jewish iron, Jewish steel—this is the concept of *Barzel*. It implies a toughness in dealing with those who would harm or destroy the Jew. It means offering an open hand in peace and, if rejected, substituting for it an iron fist in defense of Jewish interests. It means saying that the Jew is prepared to be talked to man to man or pig to pig but—never again—man to pig. It means understanding that degrading the Jewish people is but the first step leading to attempts to wipe them out.

We dare not allow the Jewish name and Jewish honor to be degraded and humiliated, for such a thing is but the first step in the ultimate plan of physical assault. Humiliation tears the spirit and the will to fight from a people and encourages the enemy to look upon the Jew without fear but with only contempt. This is what drove David to anger when he heard the giant Goliath mocking and degrading Jewish honor. Furiously David asked: "Who is this uncircumcized Philistine that he humiliates the ranks of the people of the living G-d?"

Jewish honor cannot be sullied. It must be defended from insult and degradation, for Jewish honor symbolizes the Jewish people. A successful attack upon the first must presage an assault on the second.

And Barzel means more than this. It means understanding the many lessons of Jewish history, lessons bought with Jewish blood. They are the lessons of Jabotinsky, the lessons of the Jewish underground in Palestine, the lessons of the Jewish partisans in Eastern Europe, the lessons of the State of Israel. They are the lessons that underline the principle of Jewish survival: When one deals with Esau he must be prepared to use the weapons of Esau. More important, he, must be proficient in their use. In short, in the defense of Jewish rights, property, and lives, the Jew must learn the art of Barzel, the art of physical self-defense. It is better to know how and not have to fight, than to have to fight and not know how.

"Respect and suspect" is the Talmudic admonition. The Jew must hope for the best and be prepared for the worst. That preparation must take tangible form in being ready to use whatever means are necessary for Jewish survival and defense and in being proficient in them.

How does one aid the Soviet Jew who has cried out for half a century to no avail? What does one do for him after trying all the respectable and orthodox ways and watched them fail? What is one allowed to do and what is forbidden?

How does one help the Jew who is the target of attacks by gangs of hoodlums shouting, "dirty Jew"? What does one do when pacifism, diplomacy, persuasion, and pleas for police help prove futile? What does one do to prevent the daily beatings and insults and injuries? What is one allowed to do and what is forbidden?

What does one do for the neighborhood that has become hell for those who live there and whose inhabitants dwell in nightmarish imprisonment within their own apartments? How does one help the one who is afraid to walk his streets, who trembles at the stranger entering his store? What is left after being told by the police that there is nothing that can be done and when political leaders prefer to shut their eyes lest they awaken the demons of urban riot and anarchy? What is one allowed to do and what is forbidden?

When everything else has been tried and faltered, when all that is responsible and decent has failed to help the victim of oppression and terror, it is time for a Jew to use whatever means are necessary to help a brother who is sinking beneath the waves of suffering. Those who are fortunate enough not to feel the pain of persecution or the suffering of poverty and violence should not be allowed to impose their respectability (whose genesis is a desire not to offend their non-Jewish neighbors) on people who are at the mercy of a cruel fate that is not stemmed by respectable solutions.

When all else has been tried and has failed and when the cries of a Jewish brother in distress have not abated, the Jew is morally allowed—nay, compelled—to turn to violence as a last resort. Failure to do so not only is not the path of honor and morality but is a shameful and tragic retreat from a difficult obligation to save a fellow Jew through any and all means.

And so, the training of young Jews in karate and other means of self-defense so that they will never again be the consistent targets of Jew-hating bullies; the training of Jews in the art of riflery so that the reputation of a lawful gun in every Jewish home and a marksman behind every gun may give second, third, and tenth thoughts to those who terrorize Jewish neighborhoods on the assumption that they are the easiest of marks; the setting up of anti-crime patrols in violence-plagued Jewish neighborhoods so that the muggers, rapists, and potential murderers who look upon these neighborhoods as the least dangerous for plying their trade will receive the rudest of shocks; the escalation of the war of the Jewish people against their Soviet oppressors through the use of physical force and violence in order to make the issue a world problem and to force the nations of the world to deal with something that otherwise would have been shunted aside as it has been for the last half-century—all these are things that are permitted, that are mandatory, that are compelling for a Jew, as a Jew.

At the same time, all these are things that drive certain Jewish circles berserk, up their wood-paneled walls in a frenzy of anguish, fear, and, eventually, hatred of those who advocate such policies.

There is a wailing in the streets and a shouting and gnashing of teeth. Many Jewish leaders and Establishment groups are up in arms. The issue is violence on behalf of oppressed Jews. The question is the morality and the admissability of Jewish force and power; and the angry cries and shouts that are heard are stark evidence that the Jewish Establishment is not as paralyzed and impotent as so many Jews have believed. Can these bones live? They can and do. They move and shout and condemn and struggle.

In the wake of a sudden upsurge of Jewish self-help, physical retaliation against neighborhood anti-Jewish hoodlums and attacks against Soviet oppressors, Jewish leadership has banded together and decreed:

Violence is intolerable. Violence is un-Jewish. Force is the province of Esau—if not the devil. A Jew must not stain his moral code of honor by the use of violence.

And so, when a Soviet government office was the

target of an explosion, every Uncle Jake worthy of the name descended upon Washington with a spiritual peace offering and a frenzied declaration: We did not do it! As if anyone, knowing them, would have remotely suspected that they did. . . .

Violence is un-Jewish. The Almighty and Torah and all that is holy to us proclaim that the fist is not the Jewish way. Thus spoke the Jewish Establishment.

Once there was a Jew, a very good Jew. Indeed, by now, he has become a most respected Establishment Jew. His name was Moses, but he is more correctly known as Moshe Rabbeinu—Moses, our teacher. It is an appellation given to few people in the entire history of the Jewish nation. One presumes that he was crowned with the diadem of "teacher" because there were things which he came to teach us. One assumes that we are expected to learn certain things from our teacher.

The rabbis tell us that one who serves a scholar is greater than one who studies from him. The reason obviously is that one who serves a master and daily watches his behavior learns from the most practical of standpoints exactly how he, himself, should behave. Moshe Rabbeinu, Moses, our teacher, taught the Jew how to behave in times of suffering.

It is true that the Bible commends the practice of turning the other cheek. For the Jew who is impressed, let him know that he has been reading the wrong Bible. In the Jewish Bible, we find the story of a man named Moshe who went out one day to see the sufferings of his people, enslaved in the Land of the Pharaohs. There, he saw an Egyptian beating a Jew (a thing that has become somewhat of a rarity in our times), and he acted in a manner that should be a lesson for the Jew in how to behave toward his oppressors.

Ignoring an impulse to create a committee to study the root causes of Egyptian anti-Semitism or to hastily convene a meeting of the National Conference of Egyptians and Jews, the Bible tells us, in simple and unsophisticated tones: "And he smote the Egyptian." Thus did Moses, our teacher, teach us; and whether we agree or disagree with him is not the relevant factor at this time. It is rather important for us to remember that Moses, our teacher, used violence to aid a Jew. Important for us, who have been sermonized and lectured to and moralized at by so many Jewish lay leaders and too many rabbinical ones, on the prohibition of violence.

The tragedy of the American Jewish community is the fact that so many of its leaders are ignorant of Jewish tradition, are so remarkably un-Jewish themselves. Being people with the most limited knowledge of Judaism; being men and women whose Jewish education was arrested at or about the age of thirteen, they are abysmally unaware of Jewish concepts. They are filled with the assimilated and foreign liberal concepts upon which they were raised. These are not necessarily the same as Jewish ones. The proper study of Judaism is Judaism and the proper place to learn Jewish concepts is from a Jewish source. The Talmud tells us that the "actions of the fathers are a direction for the sons," and it behooves us to search Jewish history and tradition for the proper response to oppression and to the question of whether or not violence is Jewish or un-Jewish, permissable or verboten.

There is surely not a Jew who does not concede that violence is a deplorable thing. On the other hand, there is surely not a thinking Jew who cannot conceive of worse things.

If Judaism were a religion such as that envisioned by the flower people of all ages, there would be no provision in it for war. If Judaism conceived of peace as the ultimate, absolute, and only path in life, we could not have placed in our pantheon of heroes so many men whose lives have been associated with acts of violence. More to the point, if Judaism had taken the same position on violence as so many ignorant Jews do, there would, today, be far fewer Jews around, ignorant or otherwise.

To be sure, the Bible and Talmud extol peace as the greatest of virtues, going so far as to declare that the Almighty found no more precious vessel for His people, Israel, than that of peace. There can be no quarrel with those who credit the greatness of Aaron the High Priest as being his ability to "love peace and pursue peace." No knowledgeable Jew denies that peace is the ultimate ideal, just as he must admit that, until that utopian era, we must continue to abide by the Talmudic axiom:

"If one comes to slay you—slay him first." (Berachot 58)

If peace is beautiful, it cannot be bought at the expense of freedom. Slavery is not an acceptable price to pay for a pacific world, and those who preach peace in the face of injustice are too often more concerned with their own bodies than with the souls or bodies of those who are oppressed.

What a Jew must and must not do for other Jews who are suffering is predicated upon the great ideal of "Ahavat Yisroel," love of Jew. This magnificent concept is stated simply, forcefully and unequivocally in the Torah as:

"Thou shalt not stand idly by your brother's blood." (Leviticus 19:16)

The Talmudic commentary on this verse is quite clear:

How do we know that one who sees his comrade drowning in the sea or threatened by a wild beast or by armed robbers is obligated to same him?

We are taught: "Thou shalt not stand idly by your brother's blood."

How do we know that if one sees someone pursuing his comrade with the purpose of killing him, that he is free to save a life through killing the pursuer?

We are taught: "Thou shalt not stand idly by...." (Sanhedrin 73)

And so, it is clear that the cry of a Jew for help brings forth an obligatory response on the part of every other Jew. That response is not a thing limited, necessarily, to non-violence, as seen from the provisions in the Talmud for war, both obligatory and permissive.

"And what is considered an obligatory war? The war against the seven nations (Canaan) and the war against Amalek and the saving of Jews from the hands of an enemy that comes to do battle against them." (Maimonides, *Hilchot Melachim* 5:1)

Those who are familiar with the Bible (Deuteronomy 20) know full well the provisions for war. Those who have studied the Talmud (Tractate Sotah 42-44; Sanhdrin 20; Sifri; Shoftim) know full well that Judaism clearly provides for both obligatory and permissive wars. They know that to aid Jews who are set upon by an enemy is an obligation upon each and every Jew.

"If one pursues another for the purpose of slaying him, every Jew is commanded to save the one being pursued from the hands of the pursuer even at the expense of the life of the pursuer." (Maimonides, *Hilchot Rotzeyach* 1:6)

This is surely not a paean to pacifism but rather a commandment to violent action.

"Of David—Blessed be the L-rd, my fortress, who teaches my hands to do battle, my fingers war." (Psalms)

This is not a sermon on behalf of surrender but a hymn by the sweet singer of Israel hallowing the sanity of survival.

Jewish history is replete with warriors and fighters for Jewish brethren, nationality, and land. If today we speak of a "new Jew" growing up in Israel, we make a great mistake. The tough, free, young sabra is hardly a "New Jew"; he is, rather, the resurrection of the "Old Jew," the one who first strode the land more than three thousand years ago and who fought and used violence to protect it and his people until Roman times.

The Old Jew is our father Abraham hastening to do battle against the four kings in order to save his kidnapped nephew Lot. It is our father Jacob preparing himself for his encounter with Esau in three ways; through the giving of gifts, through prayer, and through war (see the Jewish commentator Rashi on Genesis 32:9). He is Moses smiting the Egyptian and the Children of Israel going to war against Amalek, Midian, Sihon, and Og.

Joshua and Gideon, Deborah and Samson, Saul and David hardly turned the other cheek. One presumes that when Jews light their Hanukkah candles to honor the miracle of the ages they do not believe that the Maccabees were apostles of non-violence. One would hope that when we climb Masada and swell with pride we are not assuming that those who died on that mountain top were followers of Ghandi and met the Romans with petitions. One would pray that our leaders would think of a rabbi named Akiva who told his twenty-four thousand students to close their books of the Talmud and join the army of Bar Kochba in battle against the Romans.

In short, one would fervently desire that those who teach us what is "Jewish" would first learn it themselves.

No, those who fight today in Israel are not "New Jews" but the resurrected "Old Jews" of yesteryear. The New Jew came into being in exile, the tragically twisted product of fear and persecution. The New Jew still walks the streets of the lands of the Diaspora and occupies the offices of the Jewish Establishment there.

For so many years, for so many long centuries, was

the Jew a plaything for the nations of the world, for so long did we accept our beatings and agonies and death that we became a frightened and twisted people incapable of resistance and accepting our fate with the resignation of sheep being led to slaughter. And this is what the great scholar Maimonides meant when he wrote:

"It is this that lost for us our kingdom and destroyed our Holy Temple and lengthened our exile and brought us to our present plight . . . Our fathers sinned and are gone . . . they failed to busy themselves with learning how to make war." (Collection of Letters of Maimonides)

They beat us and we accepted it; they slew us and we did nothing to protect ourselves. Thus was born the New Jew; it is time to bury him.

At the turn of the century a pogrom at Kishinev shook the world. The drunken and hate-ridden pogromchiks roared through the Jewish quarter looting, raping, and murdering. The great Hebrew national poet Bialik, his hands shaking with pain and rage, sat down to write a poem of pain and rage. He called it "The City of Slaughter."

But his rage was not directed at those who slew the Jews. His pain was not derived from their action. The hurt stemmed from the actions of the Jews, and the fury was aimed at them. Jews, he cried out, Jews who hid beneath their beds as wives were raped and children slaughtered. He castigated them, the Jews he loved so much. He castigated them because he loved them so much and because he knew that unless the Jew rose to fight back with pride and violence he would die both physically and spiritually. And in a memorable line he pointed and said "Behold, these are the sons of the Maccabees. . . ."

It marked a turning point. Somewhere in the recesses of the Jewish mind a decision was made. Somewhere stirred the memories of the Old Jew and the need to resurrect him. And thus began the redemption. With the determination on the part of a few Jewish revolutionaries the age of the New Jew was over. Never again would the Jew assume his lemminglike posture. Never again would Kishinev be the symbol of the Jew. In the words of Jabotinsky: "To die or to conquer the hill."

The creation of the Betar Youth Organization in Europe was a death blow to the concept of the New Jew. Young Jews in Poland, Germany, Lithuania, Hungary, Latvia, and Czechoslovakia were taught the art of firearms. And people grew angry, and Jewish leaders exploded in condemnation: Fascists! Hooligans! What need have we of guns! Guns are not for Jews!

But the Jewish revolutionaries understood the lesson of the Galut—the exile. They knew the Polish national sport of pulling out Jewish beards at their roots and that behind the name Zhid (dirty Jew) lay a potential for murder and slaughter. Why guns? Because, they said, it is better to know how and not have to . . . But because the great mass of Jews refused to believe the worst, and because their leaders condemned and ostracized the relative few who appealed to them to teach Jews how to fight back, the Holocaust arrived in time to find the Jew unprepared and defenseless, broken and frustrated, hopeless and hapless.

But not all. Those who had received their training in violence were able to uphold Jewish honor and save some Jewish lives. If you are told that all Jews died like sheep, do not believe it. There were Jewish partisan units throughout the forests of Poland and Lithuania. There was Jewish resistance around Vilna, Lida, Kleck, Tuczyn, Luckau, Brody, Krynki, Bialystok, Wyszkow, Cracow, Bendin, and other cities. There were men like Tuvya Bielski, Rosa Robota, Herbert Baum, Alexander Pechersky, Mordechai Anielevich, Hirsch Glick. There were Jews who knew how to use guns and did use them to defend Jewish lives. There are dead Nazis who are graphic testimony to Jewish violence, and there are dead Poles, Lithuanians, Ukranians, and Latvians who had eagerly joined in informing and tracking down Jews. They, too, were paid back by the Jewish partisans.

There were Jewish fighters who wielded guns—but all too few. The rest died, unable to fight, victims of the leaders who, years before, had condemned the Old Jews who had tried "to teach the children of Judah the bow and arrow." In the end, many an innocent and simple Jew of Warsaw and Cracow and Vilna and Prague died because he had been warned against "un-Jewish" violence—and the Jew died in his traditional Diasporan way.

Had more Jews known how to fight, more Jews would have lived. Had Jews been able to cast the fear of retaliation into the hearts of Polish East European peasants, fewer would have been turned over to the Germans. Had Jewish fighters possessed Jewish guns and known how to use them, more Germans would have gone to an early grave and the incredibly simple job of moving millions of pliable, unresisting Jews to the extermination camps would have been made infinitely more difficult, thus saving countless Jewish lives. Jews did not do these things, and Jewish leaders did all they could to prevent Jewish power and violence. History will judge them all—both those who called for the gun and those who condemned it.

In every generation and at every hour it is the same. When the Jewish underground in Palestine—the Irgun and the Sternists—arose to proclaim the revolt and the rebellion of Iron, the condemnation of the "respectable" and the "ethical" Jews rose to the heavens. We tend to forget in these days when the State of Israel has made violence by Sabras acceptable, how different it was thirty and thirty-five years ago when the Jabotinsky movement raised high the banner of revolt. When the symbol of a hand holding high a rifle with the words *Only Thus* boldly emblazoned on it was unfurled, the agonized shouts of the respectable Jew were heard choking from the four corners of the earth.

The Jewish underground was stigmatized by the very same Jewish organizations that still preside over Jewish fortunes today, as "terrorists," "fascists," "un-Jewish" and as sullying the Jewish moral code of honor. The "fascists" did not care. They threw their bombs because the stench of Auschwitz was still strong in their nostrils and because they knew that only thus would the Jewish State come into being as the surest guarantee of Never Again. And because they persisted, they won.

I refer not only to the fact that the State came into being—that, too, was a victory for them—I refer to a much more important victory; a philosophical one. Those who cried out for Jewish violence, since we lived in a world that understood and cared about nothing else, won out by the fact that the same Jewish leaders in Palestine who had castigated violence and the Jewish gun now bowed to it and became both its practitioner and supporter.

If the Defense Forces of Israel practice the art of shooting bullets and dropping bombs in order to survive, and if the Jewish Establishment here agrees and sympathizes and supports such things, it is a great victory and vindication for those who first advocated it decades ago, who practiced it when all the other refused to, who were condemned and turned over by Jewish informers to the British for doing what they did. In the State of Israel's understanding of the need for a policy of violence and of the most Jewish character of such violence, lies the vindication of Zev Jabotinsky and those who learned from him.

If violence is un-Jewish, there exists today a land in the Middle East that is the most un-Jewish of all states. When the State of Israel sent its commandos to Beirut Airport to make havdala over thirteen Arab airplanes, this is hardly un-Jewish. This is sanity; this is survival; this is the affirmation of the Jewish right to live.

On the other hand, Israel quickly learned at Beirut what a grievous error it had made as it lost the sympathy of the world. That sympathy had been so laboriously gained just one week earlier—at Athens airport—when a Jew was killed by Arab terrorists. At that time the entire world offered Israel its sympathy. Now, after Beirut, that sympathy was quickly lost.

There is a great lesson for the Jew to be learned here. It is an unfailing lesson in how to surely win the love and sympathy of the world. One Jew killed is sure to earn sympathy, while two Jews is far better; and when one can live to see six million—well! Then the sympathy of the world is boundless and they will bestow upon us plaques and monuments of all kinds. Blessed is the people that is fortunate enough to bask in so much sympathy!

On the other hand, a dissenting note was sounded once by the late Premier of Israel, Levi Eshkol. At a news conference which he held following yet another condemnation of Israel by the United Nations, Echkol declared:

"Had we lost the war the eulogies over the Jewish State would have been among the most beautiful of all time. All over the world parliaments would have risen for two minutes of silence for the memory of yet another two-and-one-half million Jews.

"Instead, this time, we decided to live. So we fought and we won. They condemn us for this. But we live. We prefer it that way."

Violence is, indeed, always evil—but sometimes necessary, and those who condemn it are, usually, not

troubled at the moment by problems, horrors, and tyranny. At such times it is exceedingly simple to hold forth
with pious protestations. Those who are faced with the
sword, however, and who cry out for a help that is not
forthcoming are faced with a rather more pressing problem.

Violence is always a bad and a sad thing. Violence is
always a tragedy. But violence is, sometimes, necessary
to survive, and when all else has failed, the one who
eschews violence for self-destruction and suicide is a fool
—and a most un-Jewish one at that. And the one who
sermonizes unto us and intimidates us by thundering
"not by might and not by valor but rather by My Spirit,
saith the L-rd," succeeds in convincing us of the prohibition of force only because we are even more abysmally ignorant of Judaism than he is.

To be sure, the Jew has always looked to the Almighty, and without Him there is no hope, but the clear
meaning of the verse in the light of countless sources allowing—and, indeed, enjoining— violence is that Jewish
power and force must be used only in conjunction with
trust in Heaven. The Red Sea did not split until Jews
leaped in, and the Jewish people were not handed the
Land of Canaan by the Almighty without a struggle.
"One does not depend upon miracles," the rabbis tell
us, and man must first do all in his power to save himself and his brother. This, together with the aid of Heav-
en, assures success.

The greatness of Judaism lies in its great tradition
and in its great spirit. But there can be no spirit without

a body and all the great Torah centers of Eastern Europe that once gave forth of the Jewish spirit are no longer in existence today, because the only bodies that are left are dead ones. The Holocaust would not have been completely averted by Jews who knew how to fight back and who had been trained to fight back. A great tragedy would still have occurred even if the Jews of Eastern Europe who had lived all their lives in an atmosphere of Jew-hatred and oppression had trained well in the art of self-defense and violence. But surely, many, many of those who died would have lived and many a German would have gone to the grave along with a fallen Jew.

The saddest thing about those who condemn violence is usually their own distance from personal danger. The one who is not being beaten can rarely understand the agony of the victim of violence, and those who live in safety and comfort are unable to feel the pain of those who are daily prey to assault and injustice. It is so easy to pontificate about "morality" from the safety of a socio-economic ivory tower, but when one's own flesh and blood is suddenly placed in jeopardy, how remarkable is the change in attitude, how miraculously one suddenly understands the need for a forceful stance.

There are moralists who live in the safety of the suburbs and who unleash all manne rof vituperation against the "vigilantes" who patrol urban areas of crime and violence. How simple it is to a simpleton! The resident of a Scarsdale or an Elkins Park or a Beverly Hills or any other "nice" neighborhood can pass judgment with such alacrity. He does not have to live in neighbor-

hoods where muggers, rapists, and addicts are to the in-
digenous urban community as trees, sports cars, and spacious lawns are to suburbia.

It is not the wealthy suburbanite who has to sit in
growing dread and in mounting nervousness when her
child is late returning from school. It is not in the areas
where America has already been greened that synagogue
and community meetings are no longer held at night lest
the trip to the meeting prove to be a one-way thing. It
is not the beautiful and expensive shopping centers that
lock their doors during the day, opening them only for
a recognized customer. It is not the rabbis of the luxur-
ious temples who are in the position of the small urban
shopkeeper who goes to work daily with the trepidation
of one who goes to the battlefield.

"Who shall live and who shall die; who shall come
to a timely end and who to an untimely end; who shall
perish by fire and who by water; who by sword and who
by beast . . . who by strangling and who by stoning; who
shall be at peace and who shall be molested. . . ."

These are the words that Jews chant on the High
Holy Days. The Jew in the troubled urban areas recites
them daily. What a pity that his voice reaches Heaven
and not the ears of the safe and comfortable Jewish
brothers.

"I beg of you, dear friend, when you go back to the
free world don't hold your peace. Stir up the people,
turn the world upside down if you must, but help us."

These are the words of Volodenka's grandfather;
they are directed at us and at our consciences. How sad

that we hear them and shake our heads in sympathy and go about our business. It is not strange. It is not our sons and daughters who face national and cultural genocide. It is not our immediate kin who are on trial in Leningrad and Riga and Kishinev. Because of this it is so simple to condemn those whose feeling of Jewish pain leads them to do that violence which does so much to alleviate the Soviet Jewish problem.

Are there more important laws than the one that decrees the saving of a Jewish life *or a Jewish soul?* Are there any laws that we may not violate in order to rescue a Jew from physical or spiritual death? Come, let us learn an halacha (law) in the Code of Jewish Law:

"If one learns that his child has been kidnapped on the Sabbath for the purpose of removing the child from the people of Israel, he is commanded to immediately go to the rescue even if it means desecrating the Sabbath and, if he refuses, the court orders him to do so." (Shulchan Aruch, *Orach Chaim,* 306:14)

There may be a more important or holier commandment in the Torah than that of the Sabbath, but I do not know of such a one.

When the Law not only permits us, but *obligates* us to descrate the Sabbath in order to rescue one Jew who is being forcibly torn from the body of the Jewish people, what does this tell us about our responsibility to three-and-one-half million Jews who find themselves in this position? Since when has the prohibition against harassment of Russians or violence against their property taken precedence over a Sabbath that we are obligated to desecrate to rescue even one Jew?

Perhaps one of our problems is that we are overawed when the less learned majority cries out that the most venal of sins is daring to use violence on behalf of the cause of freedom. If so, let us remember, that it is far better to be a tail to lions than the head of jackals.

ZIONISM

Hadar is achieved through a study of Jewish history, that magnificent chronicle of a people that defies all logic.

Jewish history! That whirlpool of tragedy, drama, and courage, whose richness and color dazzle anyone who plunges into its depths. And the American Jew, whose ignorance of self is devastating, knows it not. It is so important that he travel backward through the pages of his own times! It is so necessary that he learn what his stubborn zeydes did or refused to do and how, but for their obstinacy, he would not exist today.

Hadar reaches its zenith when we contemplate, with a mixture of broken-heartedness and glorious pride, the stubborn refusal of the Jew to give up his faith either to the swords of our enemies or to their blandishments.

The list of Jewish enemies seems endless: Pharaoh, Assyria, Babylonia, Haman of Persia, Antiochus of the

Greeks, Hadrian of the Romans, Christian fanatics throughout Europe and Asia Minor, Muslim fanatics in North Africa and in the Middle East, and finally, the twin horror of our own time, Nazi Germany and the Soviet Union. These stand as a continual threat to the survival of the Jewish people, a threat which has been met by us in stubbornness, strength of purpose, and a tenacity which comes from Hadar and creates within us Hadar.

One who walks the footpaths of Jewish history cannot be a self-hater, for he finds there too much respect and pride for his ancestors. Nor can he doubt the existence of a Deity, for that which happened and that which sustained the Jew cannot be ascribed to mere mortal man. And so, let us speak of Jewish history and let us find in it Hadar—pride and respect for our people and ourselves.

If only we could gather together our youth. If only we could assemble those who are so confused and confounded and lost. If we could, there is a message we would give them.

We would stand before them and say:

Let us speak of Israel, that cat's paw of neo-colonialism; puppet of Western imperialism; oppressor of innocent peoples and center of hopeless refugees; successor to Saigon as the major target of "progressive" forces; the Zionist enemy whose overthrow and elimination would be one more giant stride in the creation of a brave, new Socialist world.

After all, is this not what we read in all the "progressive" journals? Is this not the Marxist-Leninist gospel and the unanimous opinion of the avant-garde of world liberation—the revolutionaries? Does not Mao proclaim it unto the adoring masses and does not the black nationalist decree it from his annointed mount?

Daily, if not oftener, do we not behold the "progressives" loudly marching, holding high the banner of the Sadats and the Syrians and El Fatah and the Katyusha rocketeers of schools in Beisan, and the grenade throwers in Athens?

Is it not clear to all except the blindest of the suburban Jews and the most myopic of our reactionary elders that the enemy sits in Jerusalem? Who but the most boorish of givers to the United Jewish Appeal can fail to understand that Israel is in the vanguard of the obscurants and shacklers of the masses?

Listen, you who begin to believe the inanities and who begin to doubt the legitimacy of a Jewish State. You who weep for the oppressed Arabs and gnash your teeth at the fascist Zionists. You who waver in support of Israel and who suggest that she lie down and die. Listen.

You are too young to remember the day. It was a moment in May, the 14th day of that loveliest of months, and they stood in the streets. They, the Jews; they, your people; they, the Zionists. The year was 1948, but to Jews it was 1878. One thousand eight hundred and seventy-eight years since the long exile began. You see, that is how your people count history.

They stood in the streets and waited, these Zionists. To look at them, you would never have imagined them to be part of an international cabal, hand-maidens of Rockefeller's Esso and other monopolist oil interests. Beholding the old men, and the rapturous women and the glorious youth, one might easily have been moved to consider them the farmers and tailors and housewives and mechanics and students—and Auschwitz survivors—they claimed to be.

And as they stood, they listened to a proclamation that tolled an end—and a beginning—of an impossible dream come true. The words entered their ears, filling the minds, choking their throats, gripping their hearts, flooding their eyes:

"We hereby proclaim the establishment of the Jewish State in Palestine, to be called 'Medinat Yisroel,' the State of Israel. . . ."

And as the last words drifted off into the cloudless mid-eastern skies, the fascists of Tel Aviv burst into song, *THE* song. The words were written a mere sixty years earlier; the idea was 1,878 years old. With tears streaming down their reactionary cheeks and radiance lighting up their faces, they sang:

Od lo avda tikvateynu . . .
Our hope is not yet lost—
The hope of two thousand years.
To be a free people in our land
The land of Zion and Jerusalem.

How they sang and how they rose—for just that moment in time—to the heights of immortality. And happy were the eyes that merited seeing that moment, while how sad for you that you were not there to taste the sweetness of a miracle.

And when they finished singing, with the stains still fresh on their skin, they danced—oh, how they danced. Never was there a dance such as this and never will nations know the ecstacy of such vindication.

You look puzzled. Vindication? Let me explain so that the full realization of the enormity of that moment can be understood by you and so that you may, yet, glimpse the radiance of that miracle.

Miracles, you see, are not produced overnight. They are, one might say, not miraculously created. They are, rather, the products of suffering, of prayer, of dedication, of immense stubbornness and unbearable patience. And who, my young brother, has more patience and more unreal stubbornness than the Jew?

We have reached the ultimate in stubborn defiance and patient determination. We even have worn down our G-d. "I shall not die but I shall live and tell of the creation; of the L-rd." The Psalmist who spoke these words was a Jew—his descendants have elevated his defiance to an art.

Others drove us out of our land long before the first Arab set foot on the soil there. The legions of Rome came, and we fought for our national liberation, fought with a zeal and skill that once were commonplace with us and that today are regained once again by the Defense Forces of Israel.

But we were small in number and Heaven refused to aid, and so they burned our Temple (yes, the place that was our place of worship for two thousand years before

Omar came and stole it from us). And they climbed Masada and conquered Bethar and drove us out of our land —but not before we bled for every inch and not before we clung to every rock with the fierce tenacity capable only of a people fighting for their land.

"And because of our sins we were driven from our land, . . ." and they thought it was the end. They, the nations who hated us and scorned us, and, in reality, feared us for what we dared to believe in. And so Titus came home in pomp and arrogance leading, in chains, remnants of Judean warriors. And he built an arch of self-glorification in Rome and cried out: *Judea Capta*— Judah is captured; Judah is scattered; Judah is no more. (You can still see that arch today, polluting away in the Eternal City on your El Al flight to New Judah—Israel.)

And the Jew scattered to the far corners of the earth, and the winds that blew in every nook took him with them. And wherever he went, he looked back—to home.

The Byzantines oppressed him, and he grew more stubborn and prayed each morning, "And may our eyes behold your return to Zion in mercy. . . ." The Church scorned and cursed him, and he grew tougher, praying each afternoon, "Sound the great horn for our Freedom. . . ." The Crusaders burned him alive and the feudal Christians refused to allow him to own land or join guilds, and he prayed each evening, "And unto Jerusalem, Your city, return in mercy . . ."

The Arabs drove him out of Granada and stole his children in Yemen, and he broke a glass at his wedding in order that he not forget the destruction of Jerusalem.

He was exiled from Spain and from France and from England and Portugal, and Cossacks delighted in pogroms in Russia, and he proclaimed each Passover: "Next year in Jerusalem . . . Now we are slaves—next year free men; now we are here—next year in the Land of Israel."

And the more they burned your grandfather, the more stubborn he became, and the more they beat him, the tougher was his defiance. The more they strove to drive him from this world, the more he determined to live; the more his G-d tried to make him lose faith in Him, the more defiant your obnoxiously obstinate zeyde became.

He was obsessed with one thing. Return to Israel. He was driven by it; he was a man possessed. And so, when he prayed, it was always facing home. How curious it is. Arabs, you see, also face one way—Mecca, land of slavery, city of Saudi Arabia. But Jews faced home. Sephardic Jews in Baghdad prayed to the west, Polish Jews in Warsaw to the East, the Jewish four corners of the earth turning to face a common dream—Israel.

And when he died—still in exile—the Jew was buried in a simple white pine box (this is the real and traditional "Jewish way of death") and with one other thing—a tiny sack filled with soil from Eretz Yisroel— the Land of Israel. If his eye could not see it in life, this stubborn old Jew was determined to clutch it in death.

Listen, young Jew: This is how the world determined that he should die and this is how—in his gentle, humble way—he told them, NO!

Because he knew that there was no place in this

alien world where he could ever find his peace and security, he knew that he must return home. Because he knew—so much better than we—that all the utopias and all the ideologies and all the Marxism-Leninisms and Trotskyisms and Maoisms hold no place for the Jew; because he knew that the Trotskys and Zinonievs and Kamenevs and Radeks who worshipped so eagerly at strange altars would be devoured by their false gods; because he foresaw the Soviet version of Babi Yar and the Polish Gomulka expulsion of loyal communists, because of their "Zhid" origins; because he was so much more perceptive and wiser than his grandchildren, he was never tempted by the siren call of exile. He chose to return home.

Listen, young descendent of a stubborn zeyde. Listen and try to understand the tenacity of the Jew who sat in countless synagogues on the night of Tisha B'Av with flickering candles and tear-stained Book of Lamentations, with stockinged feet and bearded face as befits the mourner for Zion and who mournfully remembered the anniversary of the destruction and sadly intoned the words: "How doth she sit solitary; the city that was filled with people hath become a widow."

Listen to all this and ask yourself the question: Was it truly United States oil that created Israel? Was it really the military-industrial complex that gave birth to a Jewish State? Was it the United Nations that brought us home? Was it British imperialism that created this dream?

There was no Esso when Jews were driven from the

land in which they had lived for centuries and to which they vowed to return. There were no Arabs when Bar Kochba went down to defeat, and Jews were already turning to Zion three times a day. There was no Pentagon when Yehuda Halevi, the greatest of medieval Jewish poets, wrote: "My heart is in the East and I am at the end of the West."

Israel came into being because it never came out of being. Israel came back to life because it never died. It was the Jewish State in the days of Joshua; it was the Jewish State when there were Pharaohs; it was the Jewish State when Assyrians and Moabites and Edomites and Philistines and Babylonians and Persians and Hellenes and Romans drifted through history and passed out of it again. It remained Jewish because Jews never left it and there was never a time when Jewish communities did not remain in Zion.

Do you think Theodore Herzl created Zionism? Not so! Zionism came into being the day that the Jews went into exile and was nurtured by every religious law and custom. Every Jew who practiced his faith and every Jew who observed his tradition was a Zionist. Herzl was merely a man whose time had come, and Jews simply put into practice the goal and dream and aspirations of two millenia. Had there been no Balfour Declaration— there would still have arisen the State of Israel. Had there been no United Nations—there would still have come into being a Jewish State. The stubbornness of Jewish zeydes can be denied for only so long.

Let us talk of national liberation movements; let us

speak of heroes. You know so much of these things, you who march for so many causes and hail so many gods. Freedom movements? For you they involve blacks and Vietnamese and Cubans and Angolans and Zimbabwese. Heroes? They come to your mind readily in the form of Eldridge and Che and Fidel and Ho, Ho, Ho.

There are, of course, no Jewish heroes of note, and the Jewish National Liberation Movement is surely a Miami Beach night club routine. Sit down, Grandson of a stubborn zeyde and learn something about your people.

After suffering the slings and arrows of outrageous Gentile fortune and a sadistic world for too many centuries, the Jew in the late 19th century decided that he had had quite enough of moving eulogies over his grave and wished to become quite as normal as those who persecuted him. He dreamed a dream of Zion, woke up with its memory firmly captured and decided to do the impossible—go home.

And so the crazy Jewish Russian intellectuals spat in the Czar's eye for the last time and went to drain ditches and plant seeds in a desert. The Arabs who had wandered in and out over the ages and who had done a magnificent job of destroying the land laughed as they took Jewish money for the worthless land. Certain Jews, on the other hand, did not laugh—the thought of Zionist militants and radicals jeopardizing their own attempts at assimilation and melting was not a funny one, even if it could not succeed.

But the fool pioneers and their mad leaders—Herzl

and Jabotinsky and Weizmann and Nordau and Reines and Sokolow—persisted. And soon, quite a few settlements dotted the land that was not quite as barren as before and the mad Jews even built themselves a city of sorts on the sand dunes near Jaffa and called it Tel Aviv, Hill of Spring. Arab liberation movements? They were not yet even gleams in Muslim eyes, but the Jewish one had come about with a vengeance.

World War I burst upon a startled world destroying an old order and bringing new opportunity to the Jewish National Liberation Movement (NLM). The Jewish homeland, arbitrarily called Palestine, was now in the hands of the Ottoman Turks, latest in a line of usurpers. Zev Jabotinsky, fiery Russian Jew, brilliant poet and writer, orator in a dozen languages and visionary extraordinaire, awoke one morning with a dream: A Jewish army! The first in two thousand years. The first since Bar Kochba's mighty Jews held off Rome's legions for three years before going under in a sea of blood. A Jewish army!

To be truthful, it was more like a legion, with several thousand Jews gathered together from sundry parts of the world. But for the Jewish NLM it was enough. It was an *Army!* And they found enough wild Jews to fill its ranks with motley and wonderfully strange people. From London's East End came the tailors who wanted to become Jewish heroes and from France and from Poland and from Russia. Men like Joseph Trumpeldor, a one-armed hero of the Russo-Japanese War and who was to die, a few years later, a hero's death.

The mad Jews succeeded in making their army a good one. With Allenby they drove into Palestine and felt the soil, *their* soil, beneath their feet. They walked the very paths that had taken their ancestors to battle so many times before, so many years earlier. They fought, they shot their weapons, and Jewish power came out of the barrel of a Jewish liberation gun before Mao could think of the concept.

Britain, clever, perfidious Albion to the last, liked what it saw and hoped to use the Jewish NLM to add more red color to the map of the world. It issued a ringing statement known as the Balfour Declaration and promised Jews a national homeland. And Jews cheered and danced in the streets because it was clear that we would finally receive justice and freedom and nationhood through reason and peace.

Well, Jews have made so many mistakes in the past in choosing to trust the world (you yourself, may be a fairly good example right there, young Jew) that we are always entitled to one more.

Jews all over the world worked for the Allied Powers. Jewish genius, Jewish efforts, Jewish money, all went to make sure that Britain would win. And when the war was over and the League of Nations parcelled out the spoils of battle to the winners, Jews insisted that their land be given to London to hold in mandated trust until the Jewish State could come into being. Britain graciously agreed to accept and the League acceded to one and all.

It is not easy to be a national liberation movement.

Freedom comes hard, as you know from all your studies of every other freedom movement. Imperialism dies hard and gives up its grip very slowly, and one does not conquer the mountain top until there is a grave on the slope. The Jewish NLM learned this a long time ago.

The Arabs attacked Jewish settlements from the very beginning of British rule. Armed with guns and quiet British assurances that they would not be molested, they struck. Trumpeldor, the one-armed hero, was shot down at Tel Hai, a Galilean settlement. His last words were: "Ayn davar. Tov lamut b'ad artzeynu." It is nothing. It is good to die for our homeland. Directly from the imperialist jargon, is it not? On the other hand, it might even have come out of the lips of Nelson, Hale, or Che . . .

In 1920 the Arabs, now the unofficial allies of Whitehall Street (which, having gotten the mandate, wanted to end the Jewish madness), rioted in Jerusalem. Along with the murder and rape that is an apparently cultural hangup with the Arab freedom types, there arose the first attempt to crush the Jewish NLM. Jabotinsky quickly gathered a group of veteran Jewish Legionnaires and fought back. The group, known as Hagana, was to be a pain in the kaftan to Arabs for a long time.

It was the first Arab attempt to crush the Jewish freedom movement, but not the last. In 1921 and again in 1929 the Arab fascists hit Jewish settlements. In the latter year, the dangerous and imperialistic yeshiva (Jewish religious school) at Hebron was attacked, with scores of defenseless scholars slaughtered. (The white flags came out quickly in Hebron in 1967.)

The riots failed to halt the irresistible tide of a freedom movement, and the Jews continued to come home in a growing tide. From fascist Poland and in trickles from left-fascist Russia they came, and from a Germany that began to reverberate to the sounds of a not-so-funny ex-corporal. The Holocaust was coming to life, and the sounds of hate began to fill the air. Some Jews, blessed with vision, kicked off the dust of Europe and returned home.

The British were unhappy. The Jews had taken them seriously and really meant to go ahead with this insanity known as a Jewish State. The Colonial Office bore a stiff upper lip and decided to kill the idea once and for all, even if a few Jews would have to share the grave. Back in the 1920s the British had arbitrarily cut off the east bank of the Jordan from the Palestine mandate, creating a puppet travesty they named Transjordan. Now they were determined to kill the rest of the Jewish NLM dream.

On April 19, 1936, Arab riots began again. This time they were not to end until World War II. The British blessed the knobby Arab fingers and closed their eyes to three years of murder, rape, looting, and burning. This was to be the end of the Jewish hope, but, dear friend, times had changed: There was an Old Jew.

Resurrected by the very soil and air of his land, he decided that the Jewish NLM would indeed have to show Arabs and British alike that a Jewish State was as inevitable as Britain's decline and freedom's triumph.

Enter another hero for you to remember. Shlomo

Ben Yosef is the name, though it was not his name at birth. Originally, the family name was Tabachnik, but that name, bred in exile, was changed when he swam to the shores of Palestine illegally. He was young, under 30; to be trusted. A member of Jabotinsky's glorious youth movement, Betar, he watched the riots and the killing of Jews. He wached as the Arabs in the town of Djani eagerly prepared for attacks on his Jewish settlement of Rosh Pina. The Arabs had been unmolested for months by the British but one night, as Ben Yosef stood on the road between Safad and Rosh Pina to make sure that Arab hoodlum reinforcements would not get through, a car appeared carrying unfamiliar Arabs. Ben Yosef ordered it to halt, fired a shot in the air. The car fled and the vanishing British were invisible no longer. They arrested Ben Yosef.

It may strike some as rather harsh that Ben Yosef was sentenced to be hanged, but the colonialists have their own brand of justice and on June 29, 1938, Ben Yosef went to the gallows at Acre Prison. He was the first Jewish NLM soldier to be martyred in the Jewish homeland since Roman times. The Jewish soil was watered with blood again; it was to give forth mighty men.

As it became clear that only the gun would bring justice, freedom and liberation, the Jewish NLM gave birth to two new groups. One was known as the Irgun Zvai Leumi (National Military Organization) and the other as the Fighters for Freedom of Israel (FFI) or the Stern group. (Please do not use the word "gang" in this connection, my young friend, especially if you are numbered among those who excuse every heroic Vietcong bombing of Vietnamese marketplaces.) They began to fight back against Arab murderers; they preferred to retaliate for death to insure that it not recur. It usually did not.

Remember their names, grandson of a zealous zeyde, for they wrote a glorious chapter in the long series of glorious chapters of the Jewish NLM. Remember the names Irgun and Stern for they may very well be among the most important additions to your educational process; they may very well be the remaking of a Jew.

They, together with Hagana, existed long before the counter-revolutionary Arab Fatah bandits. They existed long before Fidel or Che; and the Black Panthers were not even a remote concept when these Jewish liberation fighters threw bombs at the imperialist British. These were the Old Jews, the guerrillas and "terrorists" and thirsters for freedom who demanded what was theirs, who pounded the long tables and shouted: "Lamut o lichbosh et ha'har." To die or to conquer the mountain.

And so, they prepared to enter history's stage as World War II descended upon a world in agony. The Jews have known many enemies in their illustrious suffering but none to compare with the Hitlerite and Stalinist alliance that doomed six million to become ashes and soap. On the day that the Right and Left fascist flunkeys, Ribbentrop and Molotov, signed a pact of friendship, the Jew in Europe was doomed and the War of Wars was guaranteed.

In the Jewish homeland, the Jewish NLM gritted

its teeth and postponed for awhile its encounter with Albion. Jews flocked to the British and Allied side, to the side that stood in the path of the night of the long knives. The Arabs? What were the "progressives" of the Middle East doing? Anwar Sadat was being arrested for intriguing with Nazis in Egypt; a revolt was being planned by the Arabs in Iraq (the Irgun leader David Raziel was killed as he fought the pro-Nazi Arabs there); the Grand Mufti of Jerusalem was recruiting Muslims in Yugoslavia for Hitler. While your brothers fought the fascists in Tobruk and Benghazi and Tunis and Sicily and Italy, your progressive Arab friends were fighting for justice with the beasts of Buchenwald.

The British, with admirable consistency, continued to knife the Jewish NLM in the back. The night having descended on Europe, Dachau and Auschwitz and Buchenwald and Bergen-Belsen and Treblinka and Maidanek could surface unashamedly. The cattle cars bearing the Jews rolled into the camps, and the superb German efficiency converted their cargoes into dust with increasing ingenuity. The beautiful world, about whom we are told to give a damn, yawned at the sight, and a third of your people left this earth, post haste.

Some had an opporunity to flee. They did—in leaking containers that called themselves ships, inching their way across the Mediterranean to the one place that a Jew could ever again call home. Some managed to reach the shores of Zion with the smell of Auschwitz in their nostrils and the cries of "Zhid" in their ears. They managed to get home, and the British turned them right around.

One such ship was known as the *Struma*. It carried eight hundred people, and the British told them to go back. They tried to but could not make it. The *Struma* sank as it struck a mine. Two hundred other Jews on the *Patria* reached Haifa Bay and were similarly ordered to go back. They blew themselves up instead.

In Cairo resided the man responsible for administering the death of Zionism. His name was Lord Moyne. In imperialist splendor, he was the man who ran the Middle East for the barons of colonialism. The *Struma* and *Patria* were his playthings and the hundreds of thousands of Jews who might have been saved owe him a debt of gratitude for their eventual fate. Enter new Jewish heroes.

Their names were Eliahu Hakim and Eliahu Bet Tzuri. They were Sephardic Jews.

You read a great deal in the "progressive" literature about discrimination against Sephardic Jews, and of the joys of Arab Muslims, Christians, and Jews living together in peaceful unity, freed from the clutches of racist Zionists. Listen.

The ranks of Irgun and Stern were filled with eager Sephardic volunteers who understood better than we ever could the tender mercies of the of the Muslim and Christian Arabs. They made up a majority of the Jewish NLM which fought for a Jewish State. Hakim and Bet Tzuri were Sephardim; they killed Lord Moyne; on March 22, 1945, they were hanged in Cairo for their "crime." Three years later, the Jewish State was in existence and one million Sephardic Jews fled from the Arab havens—Algeria, Morocco, Yemen, Iraq, Lebanon,

Egypt, and Libya. One million Sephardim came home
to the Land of Israel.

Allow me another diversion, grandson of a long-
suffering bubbe. Allow a diversion for all those who
hearken to the Fatah fraud of a democratic, secular Palestine. They tell you that Jews and Arabs will live in
freedom and equality in a democratic Palestine. Let us
tell it to the Jews of Yemen who could not ride an animal
lest they be higher than a Muslim, or to the Moroccan
Jews who lived in the ghetto; to the Jews of Iraq, Syria,
and all the other Muslim states.

Above all, let us remember the days before 1967
when Fatah and its fellow cut-throats still believed that
they could defeat Israel in war and were boasting of the
events that would follow that delicious occasion. Those
were the days when Arabs were less sophisticated and
said what they really meant. Those were the days of
"throwing Jews into the sea" and of Palestine Liberation
Organization head Ahmed Shukairy's doubts that "a
single Jew will be left alive."

The sudden Arab embracing of the concept of democracy, secularization and multi-nationalism for Israel is
a product not of honesty or sincerity but of the well-
bruised and beaten Arab who has finally gotten it through
his head that his stupid revealing of what he really in-
tends to do to the Jews works to his disadvantage. And
so they make the Jews "Arabs" and promise them equality in a "democratic Palestine."

One is moved to admire the sheer Arab gall. The
record of Arab treatment of minorities and of "adopted"

Arabs is so clearcut that only the deluded and the deluding could accept Fatah protestations seriously. The Druze of Syria, the Kurds of Iraq, the blacks of the Sudan, the Coptic Christians of Egypt, and the Jews of each and every Muslim state are exhibits one to ten and more of Arab intolerance and contempt for all cursed infidels. Rest assured, that Fatah assurances of total equality for the Jew in a Palestine state are made only with the greatest of will power and efforts not to laugh in our faces. Hopefully, the day of the hapless and hopelessly naive, trusting Jew is over. We wish the Arabs well in any "democratic, secular, multi-racial Palestine" they may establish in Jordan, but we shall set up our own.

To return. The pendulum swung the other way, and the Third Reich that was to endure for a thousand years fell somewhat short of the mark. By 1945, the Soviets were searching through Hitler's grave in Berlin and allied troops were preparing to help their shattered enemy become the strongest West European power within twenty years. The floodwaters of Nazism rolled over Europe, receded and revealed for the first time the destruction and holocaust left behind in its wake. Try as they might, no one was able to erase the memory of the smell of Auschwitz and its fellow camps that had eliminated Jews under the banner of "Arbeit Macht Frei."

The stench filled the noses of the Jewish NLM and, unlike their gentile compatriots, they could not forget it. It was a trauma of monumental pain and it seared the soul with such ache that all else in life was pushed into the background by the moral imperative: *Never Again.*

And thus, spoke the Jewish NLM—with spitting
automatic weapon fire and the loud noise of explosive
detonation. As Judah had fallen in blood and fire thus
did she begin to rise. To the amazement of the British
oppressors and a world that had long equated Jews with
weakness, timidity, and cowardice, the Jewish NLM blew
up British radar stations so that "illegal" Jewish immigrants could slip through the blockade and come home,
smashed Royal Air Force planes on the ground, blew up
trains and supply depots, terrorized the colonialist so that
he barricaded himself behind barbed wire compounds
which the Jews derisively called Bevingrads; launched
an audacious and successful attack on that Acre prison
fortress that had withstood even the assault of Napoleon.

When the arrogant imperialists captured an Irgun
minor soldier—aged sixteen—and contemptuously flogged him, the Irgun issued pasted leaflets all over the land
that read:

WARNING!

A Hebrew soldier, taken prisoner by the enemy, was
sentenced by an illegal British Military "Court" to
the humiliating punishment of flogging. We warn
the occupation-Government not to carry out this
punishment which is contrary to the laws of
soldier's honour. If put into effect—every officer of
the British occupation army in Eretz Israel will be
liable to be punished in the same way: to get 18
whips.

The British laughed, and flogged away. Two days later, several detachments of the Irgun staged public floggings of British noncoms and officers in the streets of towns and villages. The British stopped laughing. They also stopped flogging Jews.

But greatness is not achieved without sacrifice and great goals are not attained without those who fall in the struggle. And so, young Jew, the honor roll of your people, that long and glorious bloodstained list of those who fell so that you might be alive today, acquired new names and the great chain of Jewish martyrdom acquired its latest links. Remember the names, they are your heroes and pride. They are the men of the Jewish NLM who fell in the battle for liberation of your homeland:

Shlomo Ben Yosef. Dov Gruner. Eliezer Kashani. Eliahu Hakim. Eliahu Bet Tzuri. Yachiel Dresner. Mordechai Alkashi. Moshe Barazani. Meir Feinstein. Meir Nakar. Yaakov Weiss. Avshalom Habib.

Why were there no more killed? Why, with others in Acre prison already sentenced to die, were there no more victims on the gallows? Because the Irgun determined that no more Jewish bodies would swing from ropes and that no more Jewish blood would water the earth of the Jewish homeland from the scaffold. And so, when the British sentenced freedom fighters Habib, Weiss, and Nakar to die, they did not know that these were to be the last such Jewish victims. They did not know that, in the words of our rabbis: "The righteous decrees and the Almighty fulfills that decree." Indeed, the Irgun Zvai Leumi, the righteous Jewish National

Liberation Movement had decreed that no Jews would hang again. The Holy One, Blessed Be He, was to see that the decree would be fulfilled.

On Friday, June 12, 1947, two British sergeants in the employ of the Intelligence Service were kidnapped by the NLM near Netanya. The Irgun announced that the two were surety for the three Jewish freedom fighters. Immediately, the word spread throughout the world, leading to a venomous rage on the part of the occupying colonialists. For days they searched for their missing men, and after days their men were still missing. How stubborn is the oppressor and how he misreads the Jewish determination to shatter the image of the Galut Jew! Surely, the Irgun would not carry out its threat to hang the sergeants. Such a thing is beyond the ability of the respectable and gentle Jew that the gentile has always known and loved.

And so, with supreme contempt for Jewish self-respect, the British hanged Habib, Weiss, and Nakar. Each went to the gallows singing *Hatikva*. The strains of the last words wafted into the night air of the soon-to-be liberated Jewish homeland—and then died. Three Jewish freedom fighters had been killed and the British had condemned two of their own men to the same fate.

For you see, grandson of a merciful and humane people, mercy and humane conduct are not really as simple and simplistic as so many of us imagine. The words of our sages might be engraved on our minds so that we might better understand that truth. "One who has mercy on he cruel," our rabbis tell us, "is destined to be cruel to the merciful." The Jewish NLM was determined that the merciful—the Jewish people who stood in the after-shock of Auschwitz, the refugees who hammered on a closed door named Eretz Yisroel, and the freedom fighters of the Jewish NLM—would be dealt with in mercy. The two sergeants were hanged. Not another Jew ever again went to the gallows in the Jewish homeland.

The hangings irrevocably broke the back of British prestige in the Land of Israel, and within months the occupiers announced that they were leaving. The few had ousted the many; the dawn of the Jewish State was at hand. In a little while the "fascists" in Tel Aviv would be standing with tears streaming down their cheeks.

And soon, one year after Habib, Nakar, and Weiss gave their lives for a Jewish State, their commander, Menachem Beigin, stood publicly at their graves. A Jewish State had, indeed, arisen. And he spoke, and saluted the heroic dead, saying:

"We have come to you from all corners of the land and stand before you with trepidation, resignation, and holiness. We are here to inform you that the wicked arm which plucked you from amongst us is broken and that the British oppressive rule has been removed from our homeland. The hangmen who led you to the gallows have been driven out. The land has been rid of the British army of occupation. The basis has been laid for Jewish independence in the land. The State of Israel has risen, and tens of thousands of Jewish soldiers stand ready to beat back the enemy, destroy the foe, and realize the national hope of independence for the entire homeland.

"And you converse amongst yourselves during the night, you who died heroes' deaths in our time and the Ten Martyrs of old—you who have fallen in Galilee in our time and you who died of old. There is conversation among you, the greatest conversation of its kinds ever heard in the world. A golden chain links you all. At night your souls commune with one another concerning Galilee and the entire land, concerning our eternal people which has been beset by so many enemies and has been able to withstand them because it never forsook its faith. It is not the voice of lamentation and bitter weeping which is heard when you speak to each other, but joy breaks forth from the heavens above and gladness and delight are heard in the world. By virtue of this faith there arose heroes whose like has not been seen among our people since the days of Rabbi Akiba and Bar Kochba. By virtue of this faith we renewed the ancient days of our land.

"Members and soldiers of Irgun Zvai Leumi: attention!

"At the graves of our national martyrs let us all take the oath to Jerusalem which as yet has not been fully liberated and to whose liberation they dedicated their lives and their death.

"If I forget thee, O Jerusalem, let my right hand forget its cunning. Let my tongue cleave to the roof of my mouth, if I remember thee not; if I set not Jerusalem above my chiefest joy."

All this, I would say to our Jewish youth.

Can one now begin to understand the miracle that is the existence of the Jewish people? Seeing the stubbornness and determination of such a nation can one begin to doubt its historical permanence? It is this stubbornness, this obstinate faith, that never for a moment wavered, that adds yet another dimension to Hadar, Jewish pride. That dimension is Bitachon—faith in the indestructibility of the Jewish people.

We believe with perfect faith that the Jewish people is indestructible. A people which has suffered the cruelty, the oppression, and the holocausts of the great, long night of exile which has descended for so many centuries upon it and which, nevertheless, survived each and every one of its more powerful enemies, cannot be destroyed.

On a majestic night nearly four thousand years ago, a promise was made to the first Jew, Abraham, that his people would be made into a "mighty nation." The pledge by the Almighty was repeated to our forefathers and remains a solemn oath, never to be swept aside. It is for this that we believe with perfect faith that the Jewish people—though buffeted by the storms of history and plucked at by the vultures and jackals of all time— must live. It is this firm belief that is echoed every year at the Passover Seder table:

"In every generation they rise up to destroy us but the Holy One, Blessed Be He, rescues us from their hands."

And as one marvels at the incredible history of the frailest of peoples and beholds them marching past the graves of the mightiest of empires, of kingdoms that had dreamed of Jewish destruction; when one gazes upon the glory of an Egypt, a Babylon, a Greece, a Rome, a Spain—all glories of generations past—surely the power of that Heavenly promise becomes felt in the very fibre of his being.

"Can these bones live?" the Prophet Ezekiel was asked as he beheld the vision of a valley filled with dry and dead Jewish bones.

And a million voices cry out: "They can and do and shall!" This is Bitachon.

And this survival is accomplished without allies. In the end, at times of crisis, there are no allies for the Jew. At best, nations are motivated by self-interest, and we, the smallest of peoples, offer little to the practitioners of real Politik. At worst, there is a deep and abiding antipathy to the Jew, his cause, his land. Who can the Jew trust? None but himself. To whom can he look for assurance and guarantees? Only to himself and his Divine Protector. This is enough to assure Jewish survival. That is enough to swell our hearts with Hadar.

JEWISH TRADITION

But the ultimate in Jewish pride lies in that great spiritual well from which we draw sustenance and greatness for ourselves and from which we gave unto the world to drink.

The Hebrew poet Bialik, long a man of the world who had tasted of the cultures and wisdoms of other peoples, understood it so well.

"If you would truly know," he wrote, the source of Jewish greatness and stubbornness—get thee to the House of Study. If he would truly know Jewish pride and if he would truly feel the confidence of self-respect and dignity, the Jew must go back and return to an understanding of what it is that makes a Jew different. Judaism—heritage, tradition, philosophy—from this comes the very zenith of Hadar.

The pride which the Jew feels in his Jewishness is

not an artificial thing. It is not a negative pride, but one that is rich and well deserved. Unlike others we need not create a magnificent tradition and history of greatness for all that we take for granted today in Western civilization; all the moral and ethical concepts that we assume are part of some natural law or that we ascribe to other civilizations come from inexhaustible Jewish wellsprings.

Our fathers were men touched with greatness and the Spirit of Heaven. They were men who flirted with immortality and conversed with the Infinite. They took a world which institutionalized and defied cruelty and changed it. They defied gods and proclaimed their own. They stormed the altars of paganism and raised high the flag of One. They were rebels and heretics who beheld injustice, suffering, and slavery and who rose in courage and sacrifice to proclaim: Righteousness, righteousness shalt thou pursue.

If indeed there are men today who understand that men must love their neighbors, it is because of the Jew. If there are truly those who understand the pursuit—not of happiness—but of righteousness, it is because of the ancient Jew with burning eyes and angry mind and heart filled with love for man. Our grandfather stood upon a burning mountain and conversed with G-d. He brought back with him a gift called the Torah. The world was never the same since.

There is Hadar in the Jew who gave the world the concept of one G-d who is a Merciful One and of one G-d who created man so that he might achieve holiness.

This was the beginning of the greatness of that civilization we so ceaselessly reach for today. This was the idea that was to conquer the hearts and minds of men. In this we have pride—in the concept, "Hear O Israel, the L-rd is our G-d, the L-rd is One," in the fact that G-d lifted us from mediocrity and proclaimed for us a difficult but magnificent task: "And thou shalt be for me a special people—a kingdom of priests and a holy nation." Up from mediocrity, up to holiness—this is the hallmark of the Jew.

The pagans, the hedonists, the slave masters and tyrants fumed. They lashed out at Abraham and Moses and Isaiah and Amos and Micah. They burned them and speared them and exiled them and stamped their booted heels upon them. They burned their books and banned their teachings—but our grandfathers were distressingly obstinate creatures. They insisted on making the oppressor moral and demanded that the animal that was man give way to greatness. The Books of Moses and the Bible and the Talmud never ceased their chatter and the world reluctantly and painfully listened.

And those who worship at the altar of Marx and bless him daily for having given the world the concept of social justice, blithely ignore the Judaism that preceded, by so many centuries, the Jew-hating German economist. That which is ascribed to the *Internationale* was there long before Stalin or Mao had an opportunity to pervert it, and justice and liberty were proclaimed throughout the land in Leviticus long before Marx and Lenin.

And thus, spoke our rabbis in the Talmud:

"Just as the Almighty is called merciful and gracious, thou too, be merciful and gracious. Just as the Almighty is called righteous, thou too, be righteous. Just as he is abundant in goodness, thou too, be abundant in goodness. Just as the Almighty is called Holy, thou too, be holy."

This call to holiness, the seal of the Jew, is that in which we take pride. The commandments of the Torah, which are the means to reach this holiness—these difficult but beautiful commandments—are part of the Jewish heritage and pride.

Consider the unfortunate young Jew, raised in an environment where Judaism emerged as an infantile, archaic, Byzantine ritualism fit only for the senile and the cretin. To the Jewish parent, abysmally ignorant of his own faith and sublimely arrogant in this ignorance, the Sabbath was an ancient cluster of laws that modern science had consigned to the trash heap of history. One was forbidden, this garment center habitué would pontificate with glib assurance, because in ancient times it was laborious work to get a fire started. Today, however, he would conclude, we have electricity and there is no "work" involved in switching on a light. Ride to the Synagogue or the beach on the Sabbath in an automobile? Of course, for what work is there involved in this, and only the fanatics and those whom time has passed by would still retain the ancient idiosyncrasies.

Kashrut? Every enlightened Jew in suburbia knows that kashrut was invented for health reasons. Today, however, we have government inspected meat, and so let us have another round of bacon and eggs—on bagels —to keep the traditional Jewish flavor. Indeed, a Jewish army of ignoramuses—having cast aside its Jewish head and heart—at least retains and marches on its Jewish stomach.

Ritual purity? The laughs are heard around the luxury hotels and the poor *mikva* (ritualist) is the butt of appreciative laughter. Once upon a time, the Jewish woman cleaved to such things. Once a month she would go and purify herself in the waters of the mikva following an abstinence from sexual relations for fully half of each month. And now, from the cocktail lounges in the hotel resorts the derisiveness grows into a crescendo. The poor mikva typifyes all that was wrong with past Jewish family life, in contrast to our modern concepts that have made our modern Jewish tribal unit so warm and close and loving and respectful.

Once again, one wishes he could gather together Jewish youths and say:

Listen well. Listen and learn that which your parents threw away and which the temple they built and the rabbi they bought were afraid to teach you. Listen to all that your beautiful zeyde once knew and acquired, that which sustained him through terrors and horrors that would send modern Jewish man to five psychiatrists. Listen and learn, and then get thee to a Jewish "monastery"—not for the purpose of escape but to drink deeply from that well of Jewish tradition and culture so that your parched soul might revive through the clear, cold waters of Judaism as it really is, and as it always was. "Lo, all ye who thirst, go to the waters," the prophet Isaiah called out; and the rabbis echo: "There is no water but Torah. . . ."

Listen not because we seek a generation of rabbis. Listen, so that you will recover the precious gift that we once had and that made us different and holy. Listen, so that you will find yourself and rediscover that self-pride without which no Jew can live as a man or survive as a woman. Listen, so that you will search and, once again, find your roots and discover who you are and be delighted by the pride you find. And having listened, do not stop, but go back. Go back, not to the shallowness of your youth, but to the sources themselves.

Judaism, dedicated to the concept of holiness that encompasses goodness, mercy, and peace, has long understood that which modern man so strangely forgets. If one would change the world he must first change man. Society? The world? There are no such things; they do not exist. The whole is but the sum of its parts, and society no more than the accumulation of its individual people. Each is an entity, and depending upon what those who make up the whole will be, so shall be the whole. If individual man is greedy, the whole will be no better. If individuals are grasping and selfish and cruel and hating, there is no hope for the society they make up. Change the world? Yes, but only by changing man.

The Jew-hatred of muzhiks under the Czar or under a fascist Pilsudski is no different than the hatred and pogroms and excesses we saw under the Communist Gomulka. Hatred burst forth under a Kaiser but no less under a republican Weimar.

Change the world? Yes; but only by changing individual man. The good whole is but the sum of its parts—good men. This is what Judaism knows and understands and this is the point of its unique departure. Man must be raised up to holiness.

And if it sounds so terribly difficult, if it sounds so impossible to make man better—do not fall into temptation of short cuts. "There is a road that is short, but in the end, long," says the Talmud, "but there is a road that is long but which,in the end, is short." In our anxiety to change the world into a better place, let us not make the mistake of changing a system alone. That assures us of spectacularly quick results—and eventual failure. The proper study of man is, indeed, man, and the proper way to make his society a good one is to make him good. Slow it is, but it's the only way.

And so, Judaism undertakes to make man good. It is no easy task, grandson of a stiff-necked zeyde, but since when did difficult tasks wear down the Jew? On the contrary, we revel in them, we delight in their challenges. How does one go about the job of changing one who does not want to be good or ethical or unselfish or understanding?

It is recognizing what makes man do the things he does, why he does anti-social acts, why he does hurt his fellow man. Without understanding this, there is no hope of building a better world.

No man who is of sane mind and normal soul does evil for its own sake. Man does not do bad except in that it benefits him materially. Banks are not robbed merely because they are there, any more than are factories struck by workers merely as an exercise in civil disobedience. We do the things that we do because we seek money or food or power or prestige. There are times when these things can be achieved only illegally and, so, some people resort to that.

The essence of maturity is that man should understand that not all that he wishes for is his for the asking or the taking. We cannot obtain everything that we would like no matter how upsetting or painful this failure may be. A baby is born and its world is bounded by its own desires. It is born in total selfishness and cannot grasp the fact that the world cannot stop for it merely because it is hungry. As that child grows older it learns this lesson in painful ways. It matures, it gains the knowledge that it does not rest at the center of the world and that the "I" which obsesses it does not overawe others to the same extent.

Maturity means learning that "I" must bend to the desires of others and must make way, at times, for the wishes of the "we." Some people never mature, and despite the passage of years they never learn to cope with the refusal of life to grant them their heart's desires. Life for them is a difficult thing and often culminates in their hurting other people through their inability to give rather than take, or on a psychiatrist's couch at the mercy of emotional breakdown.

It is this immature inability to harness the "I," to conquer one's ego that makes man a potentially destructive creature. Judaism does not look upon man as born in sin anymore than it looks upon any other creation as being inherently bad. Within man is the capacity to rise above the angels and to sink lower than the brute animal. Within him is the power of Free Will, the ability to choose that which is good or bad. Judaism therefore seeks the means of teaching man maturity, of harnessing man's ego and instilling within him self-discipline.

Unless man learns to control his impulse and to conquer his ego, he will be at the mercy of his basest instincts and will help to destroy and harm his fellow man. This strength of will and character, this ability to sacrifice is *holiness*. It is the creation of a man with self-discipline, of a human who is capable of possessing the will power and strength to sacrifice. This is only done by the long process of habit, of repetition. One does not learn to be a great artist by being lectured to. One becomes a painter by painting. Similarly, one does not become good by reading learned treatises on goodness. One learns to be good by doing good. One builds up the habit of goodness by constant repetition. One learns the habit of discipline by disciplining himself; one learns will power by learning sacrifice and restraint.

And so, Judaism imposes upon the Jew a system of Commandments known as *mitzvot*. They are myriad these mitzvot; they follow the Jew about and pursue him without letup. They define his day and limit his actions. They control his time and his pursuit of happiness. They teach man the maturity, self-sacrifice and discipline needed to make him a better man than his weakness of character dictates.

It is these mitzvot that demand that a Jew pray three times a day; that require he garb himself in the morning with phylacteries and don a four-cornered fringed garment; that call for blessings upon the food he eats and food that is kosher and ritually slaughtered before it enters his mouth; that decree a halt to his normal activities on the Sabbath and holidays; that order him to fast on certain days and to feast on others; that demand from him marriage and procreation and sexual involvement at times and abstinence at others; that proclaim: "In all thy ways know Him."

These are the mitzvot, the very same that the New Jew found so embarrassing and so cumbersome, so outmoded and so meaningless. Yet these are the paths through which the Jew rises to the essence of existence and to the purpose of human life in this world: Holiness.

To the Ashamed American Jew, aiming merely to climb the socio-economic ladder of the New World, whose small vision and limited concepts were defined by the material "good life," the mitzvot were incomprehensible and antiquated. He looked at each one and saw in them not cohesion but a cumbersome, restraining yoke that held him back. In an age of pragmatism, that which is not scientifically self-evident is to be jettisoned and that which is not clearly utilitarian is unimportant.

But the American Jew has no more understanding of the totality and ultimate structure of the mitzvot than the blind men who, upon hearing of the existence of a creature called an elephant, desired to know what it was. The one who touched the tail became convinced that an elephant was a rope, while the one who felt the foot was sure that it was a pillar, and he who came into contact with the sharp tusk came away with the impression of a sword. Each had known only a part of the whole structure and thus went away worse than ignorant.

Thus was it with the American Jew—deadly ignorant of his heritage and religion, his mind filled with bits and pieces of twisted facts and half-truths. His little knowledge of Judaism makes him a dangerous representative of his people. He thinks that the crude little knowledge that he possesses is enough to make him a semi-expert and he believes that the incredibly warped and twisted picture he has of his faith is an accurate one. Most blind people believe that they really know the world about them. Most ignorant men are convinced of the accuracy of their beliefs. But the Commandments are only bricks in a great structure, and only by standing back and looking at that structure in its entirety can one appreciate what it really looks like and what it really was meant to be. And the individual mitzvot all become parts of a structure whose purpose is to elevate man to holiness through self-discipline and the harnessing of his "I."

The Shabbat imposes upon the Jew that immense self-discipline to turn away from thoughts of material gain and give himself over for one complete day to something higher, to contemplate that his material prosperity is dependent upon the will of G-d, stops him from giving vent to self-desires, and forces him into a relaxed full day with his family, a day unsullied by outside influences but which finds the family, together, sharing their thoughts and the events of the past week. Shabbat finds the wife with a mate and the children with a father who shows interest in their lives, in their school, who shares with them words of Torah wisdom. On this day, the father cannot run off to fish or to play golf and the children cannot escape to a television retreat. They sit together and share a life; they escape enslavement to a material world of economic, grasping drive. How true that the more the Jew safeguarded the Sabbath, the more it preserved him.

These are the laws of kashrut that Sammy found so annoying and cumbersome whose demands interfered so with the urgings of his stomach, and which were anachronisms in these days of the Pure Food Acts. The laws of kashrut, which elevate man from the animal and which raise his base instincts for survival through eating, to a spiritual plane.

"Who is strong?" ask the rabbis of the Talmud. And they reply, "He who conquers his will." The desire to satiate one's hunger, the call to fill one's empty stomach, is a primeval and basic biological need. The body calls and we hasten to do its bidding. But for the Jew, there is something higher and more sublime. Not for him is the ascetic. Judaism has long frowned upon those who deny themselves the pleasures of life as "sinful." That which the Almighty created cannot be sinful, and it is not for nothing that the Talmud tells us that one of the questions asked of man when he appears before the Heavenly Court is: Did you partake of all the things on earth that Providence created for you?

But being human and not denying our humanity and its material qualities, Judaism demands that the man remain a human being and not sink to the level of the animal. If the beast of the field is driven by his biological needs, man must master them and harness them. To deny pleasure is abnormal, but to surrender to its incessant and strident demands is base.

The Jew who waits an extra hour or two because he is unable to find kosher food near his place of work and the Jew who ignores the tantalizing aroma of meat despite his being famished, is a Jew who is strong, disciplined and the master of his "I." He builds within himself that discipline that allows him to go without and that permits him to sacrifice without surrendering to his own demanding needs. Such a Jew will be capable of sacrificing in moments of great crisis, too. Such a person will not find it impossible to give up something for a great moral and ethical ideal. When his fellow human being cries out and asks for aid and when that help involves the need to give of one's time and money and energies, the Jew who has practiced, for years, the art of doing without and of sacrifice, will not find it to be an act of terrible effort.

The laws of ritual purity take the most driving instinct within man, that of sex, and elevate it to the greatest concept that has ever been created—love. Those laws have became the occasion for embarrassed snickers and contemptuous laughter on the part of the modern, sophisticated Jew. But it is those laws that most effectively free men from the prisons of their most driving need and allow them to use it and enjoy it but with the dignity and self-respect that prevents them from becoming slavish and disappointed.

If ever there was a more beautiful relationship than that between man and woman, one has yet to hear of it. But there is none more capable of corruption and hate. The Talmud says that "a man should ever love his wife as himself and respect her more than himself." We live in a world which confuses love with sex because it never considers the need for respect. If man looks upon woman as merely an object to use to gratify his sexual needs and desires there can be no love. For using a person implies lack of respect, and without respect there can be no love.

The Judaism that decrees that man must harness his sexual desires and limit his cravings by abstention, through the laws of ritual purity, for almost half of his marriage is reaffirming the need for man to mature and to discipline himself. A woman is not a creature that one uses. A relationship with her must be based upon respect for her as a person, not as an object. The "I" of man is told that during his life with his mate he must learn to live with her as that person, sharing with her thoughts and emotions, conversation and intellect.

Thus lives Jewish man. Bound by the mitzvot and freed by them. Guided by a yoke that is on his shoulders and that gives him dominion over himself. Only the little Sammys whose vision is limited to the animal needs of enjoyment and success can fail to understand this. This is the magnificent heritage and tradition that they cast away in their search for the good life that would be free of anti-Semitism.

Jewish tradition and heritage! A return to the source of Jewish uniqueness so that we may understand the essence of Hadar and so that we may know the will power of pride and self-respect.

A TIME FOR REASSESSMENT

The time has come, at last, for a reassessment of those concepts that Jews so fervently clutched—because they so desperately wanted to believe in them. The time has come for the Jew to understand that anti-Jewishness is a permanent part of human society, nurtured by envy, economic competition, ethnic particularism, religious teachings, and—in the end—irrationality. All the gods at whose feet the modern Jew has worshipped have proven to be graven images who have failed to give him the peace and security for which he so desperately yearns.

Hatred of the Jew exists and is no less today than it was yesterday. The Jew is not liked in America and he is not any safer because of his wanting to think that he is. It is not through education that hatred of the Jew will be eliminated, for morality and goodness are almost irrelevant to education. The demons that come forth from human jealousy, anger, frustration, and bitterness are little abated by a college degree. Nor will all the efforts to mingle with the gentile, to prove to him our melting-pot qualities, succeed in our winning favor in his eyes in time of crisis. At best we are tolerated; the tolerance, sooner or later, wears thin. All our attempts to compromise and tailor our Jewishness so that it may prove acceptable to a modern world are foolish, self-hating moves that, properly, earn us nothing but the contempt of the gentile.

All our efforts on behalf of others will avail us nothing. All our marches on behalf of oppressed peoples will fail to gain us their love and friendship. Indeed, history will, undoubtedly, show us the perverse opposite result. And what is true for those Jews who work tirelessly for others in the hope of remaining Jewish and being accepted is quite as true for those who are willing to cast away their Jewishness and find universal comradeship in the world revolution.

Whether assimilating through membership in an exclusive country club or comradeship in a Marxist-Leninist fraternity, whether through conversion to Christianity or being baptized in the faith of Revolution, the end is always the same—ultimate rejection. The Nuremberg laws dug deeply into the background of the German Jew who had long since thought that his efforts to escape his Judaism were successful, while the stark word "Yevrei" on the internal passport of the Soviet Jew smashed his illusions that in the Marxian utopia of one world he could find peace as well as any other man.

We have no choice. Like it or not, the Jew must remain Jewish, because in the end—the world will allow him no other choice, except extinction. And whether the world likes it or not, that will never happen.

The beginning of Jewish wisdom, sanity, and existence begins with the understanding that to be Jewish and to exist as a Jew is a thing devoutly to be desired.

It begins with a proud affirmation of Hadar—that deep and profound pride in Jewishness and a genuine belief that Jewishness is beautiful. It begins with a rejection of self-hatred and the unconscious desire to escape from Jewishness through assimilation of varying degrees. It begins with an understanding that the Jew must begin to look to himself; must begin to place his own problems and priorities first; must begin to understand that, in the end, the only sure ally of the Jew, is the Jew.

It begins with deep introspection of the ways in which we have been guided by those who call themselves Jewish leaders and a close scrutiny of those leaders. Is the Jewish reality in America a happy one and one that inspires confidence in the future? Has Jewish power and security increased in recent years, or has it shown a dramatic downward turn that bodes ill for all of us? Have Jewish leadership and resources been thrown into the battle for Jewish causes and Jewish survival, or have they been squandered for non-Jewish and, indeed, anti-Jewish causes?

It begins with an end to the aimless search for

identity and the casting about for roots. It begins with the knowledge that one who is born a Jew finds himself, his desires and longings within the Jewish community and that he has roots on this earth; he is not some faceless, vapid ghost doomed to roam in pointless wandering like some hapless Cain.

It begins with a thirsty drinking from the well of Jewish knowledge, history, and tradition. It begins with a return to the precious gems we so carelessly let slip through our fingers. It begins with a return to Jewish study and practice.

It begins with a genuine commitment to Jewish nationalism and self-interest and, above all, a dedication to the axiom that all Jews, wherever they may be, are parts of one body and share a common heritage. The pain of one must be the pain of all, and love of Jews must be engraved on our inner body much as the sign of the covenant is on our outer flesh.

It begins with a new philosophy arising from the mounds of corpses at Auschwitz and Treblinka, from the ashes and decay of the pogroms. That philosophy must be one that places *Jewish existence* as the highest moral imperative and rejects the outrageous concept that steel and violence are unacceptable methods in the struggle for Jewish survival. It begins with the understanding that we owe no apologies for our existance, that the world owes us more than it can ever repay, though we ask nothing of it but the right to live as free men and the right to walk as those free men in our own land. It begins with the rejection of the ghetto neuroses and fears and insecurities and with a genuine willingness to look at a world that continually grasps for the Jewish jugular and to tell it: Never Again!

It begins with a rejection of false values and unreal goals. It is not the ability of a Jew to live in an exclusive neighborhood or to gain entry into an exclusive country club that is the Foundation of Foundations for us. What value to gain entry into these only to lose our Jewish souls and identity . . .

It begins with Hadar—Jewish pride and nationalism. It begins with the joining of Jewish hands and the affirming of an oath of Jewish brotherhood.

Above all it begins with Ahavat Yisroel—the love for each and every Jew.

THE LOVE OF
JEW FOR JEW

Once there were Jewish giants on the earth who so loved their people that they dared to argue with an angry Deity who threatened to punish and wipe out Israel. In the deep pain they felt for their brothers and sisters, they held debates with their Maker and risked His anger by demanding that he forgive and aid His people. Such a man was Moses, who, upon hearing that the Almighty threatened to destroy the Jewish people, cried out: "If so, erase my name from Your scroll!"

And such a man was the Rabbi Levi Yitzchak of Berdichev, a man consumed with Ahavat Yisroel, a man whose very being felt their pain and was driven to aid them. Berdichev, in the heart of Czarist Russia's Jewish ghetto—where Jewish poverty mingled with persecution and where Jewish piety overcame both.

And Rabbi Levi Yitzchak, the gentle Rabbi Levi

Yitzchak, was an angry man who, before the eyes of the breathless Jews gathered in the synagogue, would rise every Yom Kippur, Day of Atonement, and debate with his G-d. If the prosecution stood before the Heavenly Throne with his indictment and bill of particulars and demanded punishment of sinful Jews, Rabbi Levi Yitzchak interposed himself between his Jews and that punishment. He never asked the Almighty for mercy; he *demanded* it! No Jew would suffer so long as Rabbi Levi Yitzchak son of Rabbi Meir had strength in his body and life in his soul.

And the story has come down to us of the Yom Kippur when, with the day drawing to a close and the fast leaving him weak and drawn, Rabbi Levi rose and spoke to his Maker:

"G-d of Abraham, Isaac, and Jacob. You constantly admonish us to walk in your footsteps, but why do You not, once in a while, cleave to some of our ways? When a Jew, accidentally, lets slip his tefillin (phylacteries) from his hand, he hastens to pick them up, kisses them tenderly and fasts that day, such is his love for Your tefillin.

"You, however, who as our rabbis tell us, wear tefillin that read 'And who is like they people Israel, one nation on earth,' have taken that tefillin—that people of Israel—and cast them to the earth, thrown them down from the great pinnacle of freedom and happiness they once knew, to the dust of exile and persecution.

"And there they have lain for close to two thousand years and You do not even bother to lift them up or to kiss them or to fast over them. If you will forgive your tefillin and pick them up and forgive them—it is well. But if not, I will be forced to tell the world that the Almighty dons improper tefillin . . ."

And the Hassidic legend continues that these words of Rabbi Levi Yitzchak reached up to the very Throne of Glory—to the Holy One Blessed Be He, Himself— who smiled and said: "You have won, my son Levi Yitzchak; I forgive them as you have spoken . . ."

Ahavat Yisroel, as enunciated by one who felt it and lived it.

And is this not the very essence of the Jewish tradition which quotes the Almighty, Himself, as stating:

"My children, what do I ask of you? I ask only that you love one another and respect one another." (Tana Dvei Eliyahu)

Is that not what the Torah decrees when it states:

"Thou shalt not stand idly by your brother's blood." (Leviticus 19:16)

Is this not what the Talmud postulates when we are taught:

"How do we know that one who sees his comrade drowning in the sea or threatened by a wild beast or by armed robbers is obligated to save him?

"We are taught: 'Thou shalt not stand idly by your brother's blood.' How do we know that if one sees someone pursuing his comrade with the purpose of killing him, that he is free to save a life through killing the pursuer? We are taught: 'Thou shalt not stand idly by. . . .' " (Sanhedrin 73)

There is no limit to the lengths to which a Jew must go when necessary to aid a fellow Jew. He must be prepared to give his efforts; he must be prepared to give his moneys and—if need be—he must be prepared to give more. One does not haggle over the limits of an obligation to a father; one does not weigh his duty to a brother in the fineness of a jeweler's scale. A cry for help is sounded, and the pain is felt within us. One does not pause; he races to save his fellow Jew.

But there is more to Ahavat Yisroel, even than this.

It is told that a poor man once entered the home of the great Rabbi Yosef Dov Ber Soloveichik, Rabbi of Brisk, to ask him a question concerning a Passover ritual. Since he could not afford to buy wine, he asked:

"Does a Jew fulfill his obligation concerning the drinking of four cups of wine at the Seder through the drinking of milk?"

Rabbi Soloveichik shook his head and explained that the Jew cannot fulfill his obligation through milk. He then reached into his pocket and gave the man twenty-five rubles—a sizable sum—and told him to buy wine for himself.

When the man left, the Rebbetzin, who had overheard the conversation, asked her husband: "Surely, wine can be gotten for two or three rubles. Why did you give him such a large sum?"

And the great rabbi smiled and replied: "Tell me, when a Jew who does not mix meat with milk asks if he may use milk at the Seder, is it not obvious that he cannot afford meat either?"

Few tales indicate more clearly the true essence of the Jewish concept of Ahavat Yisroel. The love of a fellow Jew means rushing to his aid when he needs help; but it means much more. It means caring so much, fearing so much for a Jew's welfare that—as a mother to a child—we anticipate and intuitively understand our brother's need.

Rabbi David of L'vov taught his Hassidim this essence of Ahavat Yisroel by retelling the story of the two farmers who had sworn undying love and friendship to each other.

"If that is really so," said one, "what do I need?"

"How can I know what your needs are?" asked the other.

"In that case, you do not really love me, for if you did, you would understand what I lack without my having to tell you . . ."

If this is the essence of Ahavat Yisroel, we can only sadly recognize its magnificence and beauty as we look at our orphaned generation and behold its absence. One can appreciate light only after being trapped in Stygian darkness.

While six million died and news of the extermination camps emerged before a horrified Jewish world, our Jewish leadership, which did indeed love Jews and did indeed care for Jews, nevertheless did not love them *enough*. It did not possess that burning passion and feeling heart that gave a sense of urgency and immediacy to their mission. How far we were from the heights of a Levi Yitzchak! It is not that we failed to anticipate their destruction. It was worse. When they cried our, we were paralyzed, and when they sought out help, we were frozen into that worst of all postures —impotency.

One of the most illustrious Jewish spokesmen of our time, the late Zionist labor leader, Hayim Greenberg, wrote a bitter article in the Yidisher Kemfer of February, 1943. The war had clutched Jewry in its death-grip, and the news of the extermination camps could not be denied.

Greenberg wrote his manifesto of despair, saying:

The time has come, perhaps, when the few Jewish communities remaining in the world which are still free to make their voices heard and to pray in public should proclaim a day of fasting and prayer for American Jews. No—this is not a misprint. I mean specifically that a day of prayer and of fasting should be proclaimed for the five million Jews now living in the United States. They live under the protection of a mighty republic governed by democratic laws. They move about freely through the length and breadth of the land. The vast majority of them have enough food to eat, clothes to wear and roofs over their heads. And if any wrong is committed against them, they are free to protest and to demand their rights. Nevertheless, they deserve to be prayed for. They are not even aware what a misfortune has befallen them, and if they were to look at themselves with seeing eyes they would realize with shock how intolerable this misfortune is. This misfortune consists of the vacuity, the hardness and the dullness that has come over them; it consists in a kind of epidemic inability to suffer or to feel compassion that has seized upon the vast majority of American Jews and of their institutions; in pathological fear of pain; in terrifying lack of imagination—a horny shell seems to have formed over the soul of American Jewry to protect and defend it against pain and pity. At a time when the American Jewish community is the largest and most influential in the world, at a time when the eyes of millions of Jews in Europe who are daily threatened with the most terrible and degrading forms of physical extermination are primarily turned to American Jewry, this American Jewish community has fallen lower than perhaps any other in recent times, and displays an unbelievable amount of highly suspect clinical "health" and "evenness of temper." If moral bankruptcy deserves pity, and if this pity is seven-fold for one who is not even aware how shocking his bankruptcy is, then no Jewish community in the world today (not even the Jews who are now in the claws of the Nazi devourer) deserves more compassion from Heaven than does American Jewry.

I know how much resentment the above statements will arouse. No one—no organization, no public body—has authorized me to make such an indictment and to publish such a characterization of American Jewry. My own colleagues may very well condemn me for my arrogance in issuing such a "diploma" of miserable moral poverty and criminal indifference to the largest Jewish community in the world. But I do not believe that there exists the person who can disprove the basic fact I am pointing to, even though he may question my right to assume the role of diagnostician or of one who reproaches "in the Gate." The basic fact is evident to any Jew who has the courage to look at the situation as it is: American Jewry has not done—and has made no effort to do—its elementary duty toward the millions of Jews who are captive and doomed to die in Europe!

If today we have no Levi Yitzchak and we do not feel Jewish pain, let alone anticipate it, and if we suffer from hatred of one Jew for another and inter-Jewish antagonisms, we only continue along a path that has its precedents in Jewish history. It was not the Roman army that finally broke the siege of Jerusalem in the days of the Emperor Titus. It was not their legions that burned the Temple and leveled the city. It was, rather, a civil war that broke out in the very midst of the siege. While Romans and Jews were engaged in a life and death struggle over the existence of the Jewish nation, that nation permitted itself the luxury of fratricidal warfare in the streets of besieged Jerusalem, a war that led to the burning of the food stocks that would have preserved the resistance.

And when the army of Bar Kochba, composed of the students of Rabbi Akiba, had driven out the Romans from their land and gained an unheard-of victory, it was they themselves who turned on each other and raised hand against fellow Jew. They destroyed themselves. It was that which opened the doors to the final defeat of Bar Kochba and the final exile of Jews from their homeland.

What destroyed the Second Temple? *Sinat Chinam,* baseless hatred. What will rebuild the Jewish people and give them the strength and power to stand up and regain that which was lost? What will help them to survive? Surely, the very opposite—Ahavat Chinam, baseless love—the love of a Jew for another that needs no empirical reason any more than a mother needs a logical and utilitarian explanation in order to run to the aid of her child.

It is time to graft that love unto our hearts. It is time to rise each morning and emulate the saintly Rabbi Yitzchak Luria who, before his morning prayers, would say: "I am prepared and ready to fulfill the positive commandment of the Torah that declares: And thou shalt love thy neighbor as thyself."

And if one is to be truly impelled by Ahavat Yisroel, he must understand that Jewish priorities must come first. There must be a reordering of all of our programs. For long enough have we plowed everyone else's fields. For too long have we labored in strange vineyards while allowing our own to be neglected. There will always be people found to fight for Asia or Africa or Latin America. There will always be eager allies for the oppressed minorities in the United States. But for the

Jew, when there is a Jewish crisis, when the Jew is up against the wall of history, who will fight for him and how many strangers will be at his side in his hour of need?

For so many months I have been at demonstrations and protests on behalf of Soviet Jewry. For all those months I stood, watched, and waited for all those whom Jews had helped—all the peoples and all the causes for whom Jews had marched so fervently—where were they and where are they *whenever* there is a Jewish cause? Now, at our time of demonstration, where are all the minority groups for whom we demonstrated?

The lesson is clear. In the end, for the Jews, there is no ally except the Jews. That which our brothers and sisters learned in Europe we must learn here. Their Polish and Lithuanian and Czech and German friends deserted them in their hour of need. In the end, the Warsaw ghetto found Jewish Communists bereft of their internationalist proletarian brethren and forced to join hands with the "fascist, bourgeois-nationalist" Jews.

When the State of Israel was proclaimed and the Arab armies swarmed across the borders to exterminate the Jewish population, there was no one who came to help. No Berlin airlift was mounted for the besieged Jews of Jerusalem. No Katangan United Nations army was sent to stop aggression and no United States police action was taken to stop the threat to world peace. It was only Jewish blood and Jewish funds and Jewish support that preserved Jewry from yet another holocaust. And if there are, then, world leaders who call today for Israeli "concessions," let them know that in 1948 the Jews made six thousand concessions—for that is the number of Jews who fell in needless death because no one helped the Jew but himself.

In 1956 when Israel was forced to return the Sinai to Egypt under United States threats of economic sanctions, she was given guarantees that her shipping lanes would be kept open and that the United Nations peace-keeping force would preserve tranquillity along the borders. In 1967 when the Gulf of Eilat was shut and Israel threatened with economic strangulation, and when the peace-keepers were ordered out, the guarantees became paper promises and nothing but Jewish blood and world Jewish support preserved the Jewish state. And if, then, there are world leaders who, today, still call for Israeli concessions, let them know that in 1956 there were six hundred more concessions buried in Jewish cemeteries and in 1967 nearly eight hundred more because no one helped the Jew but himself.

Let us cease fooling ourselves. Let us stop pretending that the struggle of other peoples for their rights is also a fight of the Jew for his rights. Let the lessons of history tell us, rather, that justice and morality call for a Jew to aid a fellow human being—that is true—but do not burden us with the delusion that justice for one will be justice for the Jew, too. Those whom we help will not help us, and the equality they gain will not necessarily be of any relevance to the Jew.

Certainly, the Jew should aid his fellow human

being, but his own struggle comes first, because if he does not help himself, no one else will. Ahavat Yisroel means knowing that there are priorities in the struggle of life and that, for the Jew, the Jew comes first. After that there is time and effort to be put at the disposal of others.

Whatever else a Jew may be, he is first and foremost a Jew, and let him not forget it if he wishes to survive. The causes of our time will find backers in due time, but the Jew must burn into his mind and heart the fact that *he* has no allies and no friends—except himself! Before we march with burning zeal for the Third World, let us make sure that the Soviet Jewish problem has already been solved. Before we bleed for Southeast Asia, let us be convinced that there is no longer any need to worry about the survival of Israel. Before we bleed for the oppressed of all nations, let us rest assured that there are no Jewish poor in our midst, that there is no Jew who suffers from crime and violence in our cities, that there is no longer the need to devote our lives, our moneys, and our talents to the winning back of alienated and ignorant Jewish youth.

Our Jewish organizations must be told that we are not interested in their pouring forth funds for others while Jewish problems remain unsolved. They must be informed that they came into being as *Jewish* groups and their reason for continued existence depends upon their fulfillment of this condition. They must be told that we are no longer interested in the tired clichés that Jewish existence is dependent upon our aiding others—

a thing that has been proven false a thousand and one times. Our defense agencies must be told that their job is to defend Jews. Our legal agencies must be told that their talents must be turned to helping *Jewish* civil rights. Our federations must be ordered to stop diverting Jewish money to non-Jewish causes, under penalty of not having any more Jewish money to give away.

We must understand that our Jewish Establishment has long since outgrown its narrow Jewish role and would much rather act on general national problems. These are far more important and prestigious.

Why should an important Jewish organization waste its talents and efforts on unimportant and non-headline making problems like Jewish poverty in Brownsville or Williamsburg when the action on the national scene is with civil rights causes and the like? A pronouncement on the Vietnam war or on abortion or South Africa may not be part of the original framework of its *raison d'être*, nor may it have anything to do with Jews but, surely, when an Establishment Jewish group makes it, it is far more exciting and far more likely to receive non-Jewish, network coverage than a simple press conference on crime in Jewish neighborhoods or the problem of Syrian and Iraqi Jews.

How much more exciting to be involved with the national issues and to meet regularly with national leaders and be spoken about by national citizens, than to remain a narrow provincial, chauvinistic Jewish organization or leader.

And so, if one wishes to understand why the Federation of Jewish Philanthropies of New York is absorbed with general social objectives rather than with Jewish problems, the reason is not difficult to diagnose. When it concentrates on nonsectarian "Jewish" hospitals and nonsectarian "Jewish" camps that are part of the whole national social-services scene, the Federation has escaped the confining strictures of narrow Jewishness. It now plays a powerful social and economic role in the affairs of New York City and its metropolitan area. It now has transcended its beginnings and moved on to bigger, better, and more prestigious horizons.

Beware the fat and wealthy Jewish sitters at the synagogue's East Wall! They will not fight the hazardous and desperate battles for the Jew in need, because they, themselves, are not in need. Nor will they be satisfied to remain within narrow Jewish confines when the real prestige and the real national glamour lies in non-Jewish national issues. These leaders need their organizations and their membership because they are vehicles that impress the non-Jew. The latter really believes that the Jewish Establishment groups speak for meaningful numbers of Jews and therefore looks upon the heads of these groups as leaders and spokesmen who have the ability to deliver votes or power or people. In short, Jewish leaders use their organizations and their membership as ladders to the higher and more rarified atmosphere of the national stage.

It is not from them that we can expect salvation for the Jew. It is, as always, the little Jew, the grass roots Jew, the one who is, as yet, unspoiled and untouched by prestige and honor. This passage by Jabotinsky in his biographical *Story of the Jewish Legion* (Bernard Ackerman, Inc., 1954) clearly exemplifies the true heroes and real pillars upon whom the Jewish people can safely rest. In speaking of the first Jewish fighting force since Roman times and of the opposition to it by the Jewish Establishment, Jabotinsky wrote of the ordinary, simple soldiers:

One cold and slushy winter evening, there was a knock at my door, and a young man, very poorly dressed, came in and handed me a grimy piece of paper. I recognized the handwriting . . . as that of a friend who lived in Jaffa. The note was in Hebrew: "This is Harry First. You may trust him."

"I come from Palestine," said the young man. "The workers there have heard that you wish to raise a Jewish Regiment; so they told me to come to you and to tell you that they are with you and that you should not let yourself be intimidated. This is the first thing. Secondly: I am at your service. I speak Yiddish and English; I am a member of the Poale Zion, and know Whitechapel. What shall I do?"

"Settle in Whitechapel," I replied, "and talk to the youth."

He rose and went. And for two years Harry First agitated in Whitechapel, in workshops, in restaurants, in his committee and at meetings; one after another he sought out individual supporters, introduced them to me and then went on with his work.

He became one of the best-known figures in White-chapel; he was loved and hated. Hated for obvious reasons; loved because even opponents admired his quiet, sincere determination and his noble poverty. When the Legion came into being he went into khaki, quietly and conscientiously served his two years in Palestine, sought no honors, seldom even came to see me. Afterward he disappeared, and to-day I do not even know where he is. Perhaps somebody will show him these lines: "Shalom," Harry First, one of those "unknown soldiers" by whom and not by "leaders," history is made.

"One does not conquer the top of the mountain if there is no grave on the slope." These words of Jabotinsky must be inscribed on our hearts and in our minds and written on the doorposts of our homes and gates. If the rabbis say that Torah, the Land of Israel, and the World to Come are achieved only by suffering and sacrifice, it is clear that they seek to tell us that every great goal can be achieved only in this manner.

If the Soviet Jewish question is finally on the lips of the world and if the Soviet giant has been forced to retreat and allow Jews to leave for freedom in their homeland, it will not be because of speeches, it will not be because of petitions, it will not be because of sermons or tepid twice-a-year protests.

Soviet Jewry is moving toward freedom only because there were Jews who felt the pain so keenly that they fled their comfortable homes and narrow personal interests and went into the streets—boldly, militantly, and, yes, violently. It came about because these Jews were willing to physically battle and harass, because they were prepared to risk beatings, arrest, conviction, and—sometimes—prison.

A small but dedicated group can always overcome, whereas a large but timid mass must fail.

Sacrifice! This is the key to the success of our efforts on behalf of our people; it is the measure of a man's true Ahavat Yisroel. How simple it is to proclaim one's love for Jews; how cheap it is to mouth lofty platitudes. But the oppressed are not redeemed by words and by empty proclamations. Salvation for the persecuted comes only by the willingness of people to act in the gut manner that, alone, impresses the oppressor. If we are prepared to sacrifice, there is nothing that cannot be overcome; if we are not, the battle is lost before it is fought.

And this is why this salvation will not—and never has—come from those Jewish leaders, organizations and classes who have much to lose. It is almost a sociological law of nature, one that has been borne out by Jewish history a thousand times over. People who have position, prestige, and wealth are loathe to risk what they have—and, indeed, this is natural. But understanding the reasons for timidity of the vested-interest class does nothing for the Jew who seeks help. Jewish leaders are not obligated to be heroic, but if they are not, they should not be Jewish leaders, for an individual private Jew who is timid hurts his fellow Jew to a certain degree, but the Jewish leader, whose vested interests prevent him from risking that which he should, can *doom* masses.

It is sacrifice and self-suffering on the part of Jews that will save the Jewish people, and that will not come from the Establishment or the satisfied classes. If Herzl, in speaking of the return to Israel, said: "First the poor will come, then the middle classes and lastly, the poor," he understood from whence comes Jewish salvation.

It is from the masses and from those who themselves suffer that Jewish heroes arise, and the Jew should not lose heart when he sees leaders, wealthy people, rabbis, and others at the top, who sit on their hands. Let him not expect much from them and let him not spend his hours and days in seeking their leadership.

It is not a new thing for the Jew. In the days when Moses first went to free his people, Pharaoh angrily increased the workload for the Jewish slaves, and the Jewish officers of the children of Israel, their leaders, and family heads, angrily confronted Moses, saying: "The L-rd look upon you and judge, for you have made us lose favor in the eyes of Pharaoh and his servants and given them a sword as an excuse to slay us." Salvation for the Jews of Egypt did not come from the Jewish leaders who had much to lose by Moses' unwelcome intervention, nor will it ever come from such as these.

It is from the masses, known fondly in Yiddish as "amcha"—your people—that succor comes for the Jewish nation. And when searching for Jewish "soldiers" in the battle for Jewish survival, it is there that one should turn. This is the Jew who is persecuted; he is the one who is the target of oppression; he is the one who is poor and the victim of crime and violence; he sees, daily, the Jew-hatred. He is the one who understands and who has little to lose.

There is yet another great obstacle in putting together maximum efforts on behalf of Jewish people and that lies in the peculiar dichotomy that afflicts many Jews. Too many of us are pulled by conflicting loyalties which prevent us from choosing confidently and boldly one road along which to march. In particular, the Jew is too often torn by conflicts between his Jewishness and his liberalism.

In the modern world that surrounds and that makes up the environment that grips us, we cannot escape the swirling winds of assimilation. One does not speak here of the total abandonment of Jewishness or the dropping of one's Jewish heritage. There is a far more subtle kind of assimilation that few, if any, can escape. Living in a world that has seen the ghetto walls fall, we become citizens not only of our Jewishness but of a wider, more universal world. Duties, obligations and demands descend upon us from other—un-Jewish sources—and from these arise problems and conflicts.

The Jew who lives in the twentieth century is the victim of many siren calls for his allegiance and dedication. He is a Jew but also a man who watches as other issues and causes struggle for fulfillment and draw him into their orbits. In short, the Jew finds that he is not an island unto himself.

Unable, therefore, to live in a purely Jewish vacuum the Jew drifts into political ideology. In the United

States he has found himself, for the very, very most part, a political and economic liberal. He has allied himself with political and economic causes that range far and wide and that see him marching stridently for many peoples and against many groups. He has tended to assume, quite automatically, that his liberal, secular ideology is quite at home with his Jewishness, and the idea of conflict between the two is simply unthinkable. It is not that simple.

Is the future of Israel's security safest in the hands of the liberal camp in which most Jews sleep? Is a group which has taken the lead in extolling "peace" as the greatest of all virtues the most reliable one to defend Israel's insistence that it will not pull back from territory until there are firm guarantees and a definite peace treaty? Are people who speak of the need to end foreign "adventures" and who urge the spending of the billions of dollars we normally spend militarily to rebuild the slums and the ghettos, are these the surest of allies for an Israeli request for large sums of money and military assistance? Will people who speak of the need for American disengagement from foreign intervention and the dropping of the concept that the United States is the "policeman of the world" so readily rush to help a beleaguered Israel, threatened with Soviet intervention? Will people who got United States troops out of Southeast Asia rush to send them into the Middle East?

Will people who claim that there is a need to end the cold war because "war is bad for children and all living things" demand a tough foreign policy on behalf of Soviet Jewry? Will the liberals and intellectuals who see in anti-Communism a foolish delusion and sinister plot demand that talks and trade with the Soviets not be implemented as a means of pressure for Soviet Jewry?

Is a mad dash out of Vietnam, precipitated by mass protests in the United States against war and military intervention, really good for Israel? What will be the effect of a peace movement that has successfully managed to tire the American people of war so that they will oppose any future American involvement in wars, good or bad, for all countries, democratic or not, even though the name be Israel?

There are many cases, and some of them are critical for Jews, in which Jewish interest is at great variance with the classical liberal interpretation of history and of what should be done.

The Jew must understand that, in choosing his political or economic persuasions, the yardstick must not be the "objective" merits of a particular "ism" but whether it is good for the Jew.

We must stop being kneejerk liberals. We must make sure that we do not become kneejerk conservatives. We must guard against automatic political strait jackets. In each and every case when we look at a political issue or a political candidate we must ask: What will be the effect upon Jews?

Not every liberal is better for the State of Israel than every conservative. I prefer the Israeli politics of many conservative newspapers over that of the liberal *New York Times*. If, at a given moment, the Quakers and other liberals pressure Israel into "compromising" with the Arabs lest a war break out, a Jew should rather prefer a conservative who sees in a strong and solid Israel a foe of communism. Tomorrow things may change; if so, we should too. In the meantime, however, let us not be used by others, but rather let us build Jewish power as a weapon for Jewish rights, and this means being careful never to allow any politician to take us for granted. We should make him pay dearly for our support.

It is *we* who have paid dearly and who will continue to do so for having placed all of our political eggs in one basket—the liberal one. Let us stop being as foolish as the farmer who always votes Republican because it has become a tradition with him to do so. There is no obligation for a Jew to be a Democrat or a Republican, a liberal or a conservative. There is only an obligation for a Jew to think rationally and incisively. There are many Republicans who are better for Jews than Democrats. In those cases they should get the Jewish vote—not because they are Republicans but because it is in the Jewish interest.

The Jew is alone in a world that has tried to destroy him a thousand times over. He has only himself and his Maker for defense. When he chooses a political candidate or ideology that would make it more difficult for him to survive, he is a fool. It would be glorious if all people marched for the cause of objective truth. They do not; they look out for their own interests. For the Jew who is so clever for everyone else and so obtuse when it comes to his own interests, love of Jews calls for a consistent political yardstick: Is it good for Jews?

This is the damand of Ahavat Yisroel. Thus, and only thus, will the Jew survive.

A PROGRAM FOR JEWISH SURVIVAL

A PROGRAM FOR JEWISH SURVIVAL

The Jew in the United States stands surrounded by his shattered myths and his troubled future. The guaranteed annual security for which he struggled so long and for whose attainment he built his peculiarly American Jewish way of life is no closer to realization today than half a century ago. Despite his socio-economic growth, he faces not only a serious threat of anti-Semitism that could be activated by a host of American tragedies, but also an even greater danger to his existence—the explosion of assimilation and alienation that threatens to rip his child from the Jewish people and wipe out a generation of the Jewish future. The problems of poverty, crime, changing neighborhoods, and reverse discrimination that affect millions of his compatriots have not been met properly; Jewish leadership remains a sometime thing, disjointed, timid, and unreceptive to Jewish needs.

There is trouble in the Jewish paradise, and the Jew,

sensing a loss of purpose and meaning to his life, lacking deep roots and a sense of identity, seeks solutions. He seeks a program for Jewish survival both physically and as a Jew.

The beginning of this Jewish wisdom lies in the regeneration of the Jew, as a Jew. It entails replanting within him the seeds of Hadar—pride, nationalism, self-respect, and clear Jewish identity. It demands the flowing from this Hadar of Ahavat Yisroel—the love of fellow Jews, the feeling of their pain and the setting out to alleviate that pain. It decrees the acceptance of a program for survival that calls for Jewish strength, both moral and physical.

Without this pride, national identity, and ties of peoplehood, the Jew faces not only his own spiritual and cultural disappearance as a distinct entity before the onslaught of assimilation and apathetic alienation but also collapse and destruction before the forces of anti-Semitism; for, loss of Jewish pride and identity leads to a refusal to see and to recognize the escalating danger. Self-delusion and false optimism over Jewish integration into society and Jewish stability and security therein lead to a failure to recognize the common bond and common danger facing all Jews and a consequent refusal and failure to join together in unified efforts to stop the flood.

END THE SPIRITUAL THREAT TO THE JEW

To implant into ourselves and into our youth Hadar and Ahavat Yisroel becomes the immediate, critical priority. It is the foundation of a Jewish program for survival that calls for both moral and physical Jewish power.

It must begin with the reordering of our priorities and the gathering of Jewish assets, energies, efforts, and moneys into a unified effort to meet Jewish problems. The federations that control Jewish funds throughout the country must become democratized and committed to the really important and strictly Jewish programs. The first priority, the one that will insure us a generation that is filled with Hadar and Ahavat Yisroel, is to set aside the lion's share of Jewish philanthropic funds for Jewish education.

It would be difficult for a writer of fiction to paint a scenario as absurd as the one involving the Jewish Establishment, the Jewish Day School, and the young American Jew. No one would give credence to a plot wherein wise and distinguished leaders see the destruction of the future as millions of Jewish youth drift away into the Elysian fields of apathy, disinterest, and alienation and still refuse to support the surest and, perhaps, the only answer to that drift—Jewish education.

Nevertheless, that is precisely what is happening as old and reactionary Jewish leaders and bureaucrats find funds for any nonsense, but only a pittance for Jewish survival through knowledge and pride. It is not the "Jewish" hospital that will preserve Jews twenty-five years from now, nor will the community center basketball team. A minimum of 25 percent of *all* Jewish communal funds must be set aside by federations for maximum Jewish education. By this is meant the Day School movement and not the one- or three-times-a-week after-hours religious school that is the bane of Jewish educational existence in America and the cause of its spiritual bankruptcy. Federation funds set aside for these schools are, for the most part, moneys flung down a rat hole. If they are continued to be alloted they must remain totally separate from the 25 percent of the budget set aside for meaningful and maximum Jewish education. If federations are unwilling to reorder their priorities, community pressure must be placed upon them. Failing all else, contributions ordinarily given them should be withheld and given instead to Jewish education directly.

Scholarships must be set aside for the deserving disadvantaged or for those who desire to attend Day Schools but whose parents are unwilling or unable to pay. These scholarships should be granted from funds raised by federations as well as from synagogues which should all pledge themselves to a number of such stipends.

An end must be put to the suicidal attacks upon various plans for government aid to the hard-pressed parochial schools. These plans include both state aid to the secular aspects of the curriculum as well as aid to the student himself, whether directly or through tax deductions for the parents. Jewish Establishment groups who fight such aid under the tired and ridiculous notion that this violates their own strict construction of Church and State must be brought to heel and told by their members that they will not stand for an assault on Jewish educational survival by, of all people, Jewish defense organizations. Refusal to listen should bring wholesale resignations from the Jewish groups by their members.

There is ample reason to believe that many of the plans drafted by the federal government and various state legislatures to assure the survival of the parochial school are constitutional. Certainly, it is not up to the Jewish organizations to lead the race into court. At a time when Jewish youth is starving for lack of spiritual and educational nourishment; when Jewish Day Schools face the specter of bankruptcy that looms because of inflationary rises in costs and recession-induced drops in contributions; when these factors force yeshiva tuition to skyrocket to a point where only the wealthy can afford them—it is obscene that Jewish groups should lead the battle against government efforts to help Jewish parochial schools survive. The reactionary Jewish opponents of maximum Jewish education must be prevented from helping assimilation take its toll of future Jewish youth; Jewish efforts must be directed to demanding government aid for struggling yeshivas.

The schools themselves, the programs given to Jewish youth, must be revised to include the kinds of courses that will create historical pride and self-respect. Both in the Day Schools and the after-hour synagogue classes there should be courses in Jewish pride, with the emphasis on the beauty of Jewish tradition and heritage (without the hypocritical subversion of religious practice); the history of *both* Jewish suffering and resistance through the ages (with emphasis on Jewish resistance against tyranny and the Jewish national liberation movement throughout the centuries); the creation of the miracle called the State of Israel with an in-depth study of the Holocaust, the Jewish partisans and resistance in Nazi Europe, and the Jewish underground in Palestine.

Present day Jewish problems must be brought alive for students, and the Jewish child taught that those problems are his to solve. The story of the Soviet Jew must be taught as a regular course, and the student's lesson followed up with school-planned and led demonstrations. The fortunate Jewish youngster must be taken on trips—not to a zoo or a picnic—but to Jewish urban areas where he can see the problems of his poor and deprived fellow Jew. This should be followed by programs of action by the school and community to solve the problems that their youngsters have just been taken to see.

Jewish tradition should be emphasized so that the Jewish youngster can know enough to make an intelligent choice for himself in future years. One can always, and quite easily, decide to be an alienated or nonpracticing Jew, but one should at least know what the other side of the coin is—what he is throwing away.

Jewish heroes and martyrs must be brought to the attention of Jewish youngsters, and their pictures and biographies made available to them. Anniversaries of their deaths should be observed and a special week or month set aside for a period of Jewish pride. Inexpensive books on Jewish pride, heritage, and resistance should be made available so that the Jewish home may have its own small library of Jewish identity and pride.

Demands for Jewish Studies should be made in colleges and in high schools throughout the country, and in those schools where other ethnic studies are allowed and a request for a Jewish one rejected, peaceful protests and demonstrations should be held by parents of the community.

Experiments should be made with unorthodox kinds of methods of reaching uncommitted Jewish youth. It is evident that, on campuses, the Hillels have failed to win into their buildings the large numbers of Jewish students that attend college campuses. It becomes necessary, therefore, to create near these campuses and near high schools, Jewish Identity Centers where young Jews can walk in and discuss their Jewishness or lack of it with trained activist Jews who understand what they seek and who can help them find their own path to Jewishness. These Identity Centers should have formal classes and informal discussion groups, with libraries of books and films on Jewish pride.

Above all, they should be placed where activities on behalf of Jews are planned and carried out. From these Identity Centers the young Jew should be able to learn about Soviet Jewry and also participate in a demonstration for Russian Jews. He will only learn to respect the things he learns at these centers if his teachings are put into practice by those who do the teaching.

On campuses, continuous Jewish identity must be stressed with tables of literature dealing with Israel, the Soviet Jewish issue, Jewish identity, pride, and tradition —available free for all those who desire it.

Jewish leaders and groups cannot wait for young Jews to come to them; they must go out to the campuses and sit and talk with the youth.

We must not wait and watch as Arab propaganda floods the campuses, doing more harm against the State of Israel than ten Egyptian divisions. It is not only that some students become Arab sympathizers but that vast numbers become "neutral." Inundated by the flood of Arab arguments, almost all well written, substantively good, and of the most professional and slickest form, thousands of students begin to "understand" the Arab side and are detoured to a middle-of-the-road position that sees good and bad in both Israel and Arab camps. The result is a blasé rendition of a "plague on both your houses." The Arabs ask for nothing more than this. If the future generation of Americans, if the future leaders of Israel's strongest ally can be neutralized, this in itself is a victory of the greatest magnitude.

We must not wait for leftists to flood the campuses with their siren songs that rip away Jewish youth with their attacks upon Israel as "lackey of imperialism," "aggressor," and a "fascist, racist state."

We must not wait for an Arab or a leftist teach-in against Israel before we panic and seek solutions. That is the Jewish curse, a myopia that hovers over us and that blinds us to problems until they are upon us, ready to devour us. Only then do we suddenly wrench ourselves free from our paralysis. Only then do we begin rushing about in a frenzied panic seeking a solution to our misfortune, a solution that was mocked by us in yesteryear when there was time. Now, we realize our error. Now we repent. Usually, it is late.

The campuses must become regular havens for Jewish identity and demonstrations. Let Jewish students take the offensive and hold their own teach-ins on behalf of Israel or Soviet Jews or Jews in Arab lands or Jewish identity. Let every significant date serve as opportunities for ceremonies or rallies on campus. Let the names and pictures of Jewish national liberation heroes be as famous —and more so—than those of other world figures.

All these are the roads to Jewish knowledge, and Jewish knowledge is the key to Jewish pride and love of people. They cost money, but the Jew can find the money; it is there. He needs only to direct it away from nonsense and non-Jewish causes. If he understands the urgency of the need he will do it.

Jewish knowledge. Jewish pride. Jewish self-respect. Jewish identity. A history upon which to look back proudly; a present in which to struggle idealistically; a future to point to ecstatically. Give these to the young Jew and he will not need to wander aimlessly and desperately seeking meaning to his life. He will not be forced into strange causes and into the strange temples of exotic religions. He will not be driven to seek himself and to search himself out. He will not stop every exotic cause and every wierd creature to ask: "I am lost. Where is the road home?"

He will not be propelled into a world of drugs that turns him away from reality that is empty for him. In the end, all the admonitions and all the graphic proofs of the horror of drugs can mean nothing to a youth who leaped into the flames of addiction because there was nothing positive or meaningful to his life. Give him meaning and he will not need his drugs. Give him a cause for which to fight and he will not run away to the safety and escape of narcotics. Tell him who he is and he will not have to find himself in madness.

Jewish education; maximum, vibrant, and unashamed. This will ressurect Hadar and Ahavat Yisroel. This will water and revive a parched and spiritually barren Jewish desert. This will save generations born and unborn; these who are with us today and those who are not yet here.

STOP THE PHYSICAL THREAT TO THE JEW

And then there is the great issue of the physical survival of the Jew and the threat to that survival.

Throughout the world, Jewish minorities, wherever they may be, are under growing attack. Dark clouds appear on all horizons. The death of six million Jews has in no way lessened the thirst of a world for Jewish blood. Deep insecurity and impending tragedy loom for Jews within the Soviet Union and Eastern Europe, through Latin America, in France, perhaps most dangerous of all is the potential situation in the United States—the heartland of World Jewry with, ironically, six million Jews.

We need not repeat, at any length, the awesome problems that jointly and severally comprise a powder keg that awaits only a spark to set off an explosion that will decimate the American democratic way of life that so many condemn but that too few appreciate for its nobility and freedom within sanity. They are a volatile combination that could bring another and greater holocaust for the American Jew.

The racial tension, the social anger and bitterness, the political and military frustration and insecurities, gnawing and galloping inflation compounded by worsening economic recession, all the jealousness and envy of people directed at the eternal scapegoat, the Jew; the dark cloud becomes a familiar one.

It becomes a frightening one and a real one because of the haters who feed upon it, and who bask in its darkness. The Radical Right ticks off the crises and blames each and every one upon the Jew.

It is not ashamed to speak of its plans for Jews—elimination. Some are bold enough to speak of gas chambers. The Radical Left and militant racial extremists join together, their hostility to Jewish power unconcealed and their determination to destroy that economic and political strength, clearly revealed. Not only do they themselves pose a threat to the Jew, but by their mad speeches and acts, they bring millions of people, ordinarily decent, into the arms of the Right. They are a boon to the Right and are its greatest ally in the drive for a fascist, totalitarian America.

Still, there are those who laugh and there are those

who grow angry at this "pandering to fear" and there are those who grow violent in their attacks—not upon the threat to the Jew—but upon those who warn of it. And they shout: "Are you mad? Is such a thing possible in a land such as this? This is a land of democracy and of justice? This is not Germany." And once again the cloud is ignored and the Jew refuses to reach for his umbrella. Once again he risks deadly pneumonia.

Forty years ago, as the cloud of Nazism appeared on the horizon, men like Jabotinsky raced from town to town in Europe pleading with Jews to realize what was coming, pleading with them to leave for Palestine where the doors were still open. The vast majority of Jews ignored the warning, laughed at them, grew angry at them, attacked them. They were attacked as demagogues and as irresponsible and as men who were, themselves, causing anti-Semitism. Do not listen to them, Jews were told by the bureaucrats; stay here. All will be well. And the Jews stayed—and died.

Never again. Never again must we make the same tragic error of refusing to believe that a holocaust can sweep up the Jews wherever they may be and that hatred of the Jew is a thing that flourishes in all types of climates and regions. It is a hardy thing.

Perhaps, indeed, in the end all will be well. But in the marrow of my bones, I feel that disaster looms. And feeling this and sensing it and seeing all the painful realities that are self-evident to all who would only see, an attempt must be made to make Jews understand that the problem exists and is a real one. Above all, we call upon them to begin immediately to make concrete plans to leave and go to live in the land of Israel. There is no solution that is a better one. There is no way that offers greater assurance of the physical safety of the Jewish people in the Galut. We who flee from neighborhood to neighborhood and from city to city seeking safety and security, must stop. It is time for one last, permanent move—back home, back to Israel.

The growing madness, the growing rage, the growing storm gives no assurance of being able to be stopped. It is Aliyah—immigration to the land of Israel, to the Jewish homeland—which offers the surest hope. But one of the greatest tragedies of our times is the failure of Jewish leadership to proclaim the dangers facing us and to push Aliyah with all their might and all their resources. Can it really be that we have learned nothing from history, that the result could be, once again, a holocaust? G-d fordid.

There is still time today. There is still time while the Jew can leave with dignity and honor and with the fruits of his toil. But tomorrow? Watchman, what of the night? What will the new day bring?

It is time to use our resources to mount a massive campaign for Aliyah. Every synagogue and every Jewish institution must be a center armed with information and with aid. Hebrew language centers (ulpanim) should be established in every community so that the great language barrier can be overcome. Students must be clearly and correctly told which fields of endeavor and which occupations are needed in Israel so that they may

easily acclimate themselves there. Community investment pools must be created so that businessmen or others
whose professions and occupations find few opportunities in Israel, can find honorable and regular employment. Efforts should be made so that parts of whole communities may emigrate together and plans developed to
build cooperative housing developments where they may
jointly live. A campaign for One Million Jews to Israel
must be mounted and given the same sense of urgency
we find when collecting one hundred million dollars for
Israel.

American-style high schools and colleges must be set
up in Israel where our children can be sent while still
young enough not to be corrupted by the flesh pots of
materialism. Scholarships must be granted those whose
parents cannot afford the tuition. We must begin to build
the concept of Aliyah in fresh, idealistic young minds.

And for those who cannot or who will not go, for
those who understand and yet do not understand, who
see but not fully, who sense but are not yet fully convinced, let them at least create for themselves a stake in
the Jewish state by taking the first step to planting roots.
Let those who do not go purchase apartments so that
they may have a tangible piece of the land. Let them
place a modest sum of money in a savings account in the
Jewish State. Let them make the first halting steps that
must be taken before they can properly walk with confidence and let them insure against a possible day when
it may be forbidden to remove money from the United
States, as is already the case in many other countries.

We Jews are obligated to serve with all our heart and all our soul and all our might, the land in which we live. The law of the land is the law for the Jew and while he is a citizen of any nation he must serve it, work for it, fight for it, and honor it. That is Jewish Halachic teaching; that is Jewish law. While we live away from Israel our loyalty is to the land of our residence. Jews need no lesson in loyalty from anti-Semites.

But in the end, there is a Jewish home and a Jewish domicile and a land where the Jew can lay his head to rest and his soul to peace and where his children can cease being a minority of zhids or kikes. We love the lands that gave us freedom and must repay that kindness with all that we have. But, when all is said and done, one must go home; and especially when one senses that his visit begins to lose its sheen. It is time to go home to Israel because the cloud grows darker and the tension less bearable and the danger greater.

Those people who subscribe to the Devil theory of Germany and who prefer to believe that Nazism was an aberration limited to a peculiar type of people, a sickness that cannot occur elsewhere, are mistaken. Germany was a land of immense culture and scientific development, of humanism and progress, of people who were decent and charming and civilized, of people who were friendly and helpful to their Jewish neighbors. The Jewish community must bend its efforts and its resources toward its own preservation and must create the tools of Aliyah so we may be guaranteed that that which happened once before in our lifetime will never happen again.

And having said all that, perhaps one thinks that this ends the tale. We have said that the solution to the problem of Jewish physical survival is emigration to Israel. There is an air of finality about such a thing. What else is there to say? There is more.

It would be immensely simple to say that it appears more and more probable that terrible times are coming for the American Jew; that this demands his Aliyah to Israel; that those who listen are to be blessed; that we can only warn and leave ourselves. But that is not the way of Ahavat Yisroel.

It is rather clear that most American Jews are not prepared to go anywhere. They do not really believe that they are in danger and even those who are uneasy are frozen by the uncertainty of moving to a strange land and the insecurities of starting a new life, and so convince themselves that things will eventually turn out well. What does one do in such a case? Does one leave such Jews to their own devices? Is there no obligation that we owe them? Indeed, there is, and this is why a Jew who knows that the only solution to the Jewish problem of physical survival is Aliyah to Israel, must attempt in every way to assure the survival and security of the Jew who remains in exile. It is the mark of the Jew who truly loves his fellow Jew that he will work to prove himself wrong. He will toil on his behalf so that his own dire prediction may never come about.

He sets about to disprove the anti-Semite who claims that Zionists and Jewish nationalists have a stake in persecution of the Jew in exile since this drives them to

Israel. All the Zionism and all the Jewish nationalism in the world is not worth the death of a single Jew at the hands of an anti-Semite in a pogrom even though that attack stimulates Jewish emigration to Israel. It is far better that the Jew who warns against Jewish existence in exile be shown to be wrong than be proven right at the cost of Jewish tragedy.

We must, therefore, postulate a program for physical Jewish survival in the exile so that those who remain will endure or, at least, gain time in which to become convinced.

If the ultimate threat to Jewish survival comes from the existence of powerful extremist groups who will reap the whirlwind of hate, frustration and fear of our times, it is imperative that the Jew mount a massive and total war on these groups and their existence.

The Jew will never be able to stand up to the total strength of the state should its apparatus fall into the hands of the Haters. In such a case, no amount of Jewish defense groups will save the vast majority of Jews. It is this very realization that should make us understand the necessity for an immediate activist response while the extremist threat is still able to be met. It may not be popular with liberals and it may shock the orthodox and rigid doctrinaires, but it is clear that in a society which is increasingly polarized and whose middle ground is daily eroded while the extremist Haters gain strength, a ban on or legislation against extremist groups that preach hatred and destruction of other groups and peoples is the only solution. It is the only guarantee that such groups will not achieve power.

Does freedom include the right to speak, organize, influence, and work to destroy that freedom? Does democracy countenance the right of an authoritarian to use its very processes and its guarantees to bury it? Does it grant freedom to one so that he may take away anothers freedom. Yes, say some. For this is the view of the liberal intellectual of our time. Despite the fact that throughout the United States, totalitarian groups dedicated to the overthrow of freedom, grow stronger and bolder; despite the fact that they will, if given the opportunity, gas Jews, deport Negroes, and render the rest pitiful slaves—despite all this, the intellectual invokes the right of freedom for those who would destroy it.

They defend the inalienable right of people to preach the destruction of other people, to invoke freedom to destroy freedom, to preach and promote revolution in the establishment of a tyranny which will deprive others of the rights of democracy. They declare that no matter how heinous one's belief, he has the right to advocate that belief, to persuade others to that belief, and that the least infringement of this right is the beginning of the end of a democracy. It is not a new argument. Liberals in Germany and Italy argued so as they defended Hitler's and Mussolini's rights to destroy their countries. One presumes they had some misgivings as they were carted off to concentration camps.

History is full of quixotic visionaries, muddled liberals, and foolish children who proclaimed the freedom of men to destroy freedom, and who declared their intentions to defend that right to the death. Generally, their wish was fulfilled. The blood of countless innocent victims flow through the sea of history—victims of tyrants and confused democrats who helped those tyrants to power.

The naive belief that somehow the people will always see the truth and, following it, reject the men of evil, has been refuted a hundred, nay, a thousand times —not the least in our days. Where was the good judgment of the German who voted for Hitler? Where was the good sense of the Italian as he cheered the rape of Ethiopia? Why do one-third of the Italian people vote Communist, and why do the Cuban peasants idolize Castro?

There can never be a guarantee of democracy, there can never be an assurance of people choosing freedom. It is self-interest that guides us, and who is to say where it will lead us in the future? Who can be sure of the temper of the people in a time of economic crisis? Who is willing to guarantee Rockwell's rejection? or the Black Panthers'? or the Weathermen's? or George Wallace's?

The tyrants and racists who succeeded in destroying half of Europe, did so through the blindness of those who learned nothing from history. I am sick, because it is happening all over again through the immaturity and madness of children influenced by our confused intellectuals.

In the United States, the liberal sacred cow is the "clear and present danger" doctrine. The trauma called Auschwitz rejects it totally. It is a doctrine which was not always the law of the land. Once, in a profound opinion—

a majority opinion—a forgotten justice of the court spoke these words: "The state cannot reasonably be required to measure the danger from every such utterance in a nice balance of a jeweler's scale. A single revolutionary spark may kindle a fire that . . . may burst into a sweeping and destructive conflagration. . . . Factually, the legislature has the authority to forbid the advocacy of a doctrine designed to overthrow the government without waiting until there is present and imminent danger of the success of the plan advocated. If the state were compelled to wait . . . then its right to protect itself would come into being simultaneously with the overthrow of the government when there would be neither prosecution, officers nor courts for the enforcement of the law" (Mr. Justice Sanford in the case of *Gitlow* v. *New York*.)

Such a view, in regard to those who preach the persecution or destruction of a group or religion, simply states that they have no right to demand that which they would not grant unto others. Nations such as Great Britain and Canada, true democratic nations, ban utterances of hate and thus attempt to put an end to hate and extremist groups before they become a clear and present danger. Anti-hate legislation, group libel bills, and general bans on groups who would not grant freedom to others, should they have power, are proper and legitimate tools of a democratic society. No democracy has the obligation to commit suicide. If one feels that by giving rope to the extremist groups they will hang themselves, he has only to look at the Germany of 1933 when a nightmare was voted into power by the people. When otherwise decent people embittered by inflation and depression, unemployment and hunger, defeat in war and dismal fear of Communist revolution at home, went to the polls and, knowingly, elected a man who had promised to eliminate the Jew.

Every man must be allowed to speak and propagate his views but only on the condition that he grant unto others the democratic rights that he demands for himself. One has no obligation to give freedom to the man who informs him that he will attempt to convince people to give him power so that he might gas him. One who does so is not a liberal but a fool.

At the same time, the Jew must be ever alert to the slightest manifestation of anti-Semitism. He must move quickly against it. Italians move swiftly at what they consider the slightest slur against them. Blacks are quick to move against what they consider to be racism. The Jew must be no different. He must learn to cultivate tolerance of people who are different and intolerance of people who are potential mass murderers. The Jewish community must rid itself of the idea that small cancers can be safely ignored and that we need not concern ourselves with minor manifestations of hate.

In these days of tension and danger, of a polarized society ripped apart by violence and hate, there is no such thing as a "little" anti-Semitism or a "little" hate. Extremism breeds and multiples. Under the proper conditions it moves from a relatively small group to power with amazing speed. Precisely because nothing will avail us should extremism capture power, the threat must be dealth with quickly and effectively.

Those groups and those politicians who play a numbers game with us by declaring that the extremist groups
are small, do us a disservice. They dig the Jewish grave.

Manifestations of a Jew-hatred must be met with
angry protests and large demonstrations because the
Haters who are on the fringe wait and watch to see what
will be the public's reaction. If there is silence, the Haters
will be emboldened. They will gain the new converts
who would otherwise be frightened off by an angry reaction. They will gain the new opportunities that would
have been denied them by a government impressed by a
furious Jewish reaction. It is not enough to merely keep
copious files on the Haters. Action, immediate and militant, must be taken in order to keep them under the rocks
they inhabit when they feel endangered.

Finally, there is a need for a bold new program whose
importance cannot be overestimated. It is time that the
Jew moved to establish close and regular contacts and
dialogues with the people who, in the end, will have the
most bearing on the future of the American Jew. These
are the people who represent the American majority, the
working class, the ethnic populations, the blue collar and
the nonintellectual groups.

The final arbiter of the American judgment and, in
particular, the American Jewish fate, will not be the
handful of upper-class intellectuals, the liberal political
and social leaders with whom Jewish leadership has cast
its lot. It is not the people whom we meet at the brotherhood banquets or the individual celebrity whom we

award a plaque for his tolerance and work on behalf of human relations. In the end, these people speak for precious few others and their influence in times of ultimate crisis will be negligible.

It is rather that group that so many more "gifted" intellectuals and liberals derisively, mockingly, and patronizingly refer to as the "silent majority." Well, they are indeed a majority and they do represent the thinking, tastes, opinions and emotions of more citizens than do their critics and detractors. And while they have, to be sure, been silent in the past they are less so today and will be far less so tomorrow. Worse, I fear that their new-found voices will be angry, shrill, and bitter.

They have been neglected for too long by a Jewish leadership which did not consider them to be of importance in shaping national trends or in being any meaningful factor in the Jewish future. Too often, because of inherent conservatism, they were branded and labeled as opponents of liberal and progressive thinking and thus unworthy of being partners in any dialogue. The huge ethnic groups that compose so much of this group were ignored because we really believed our own myth of a melting pot and we assumed that Jews and all other ethnics would see quickly a melting process that would lead to the weakening of feelings of special identity and an eventual disappearance of particularism as a meaningful emotion.

But, we are wrong. There is no melting pot and the trend, if anything, is back to a fierce desire for self-identity and pride on the part of ethnic groups. It is not strange. Crises always find internationalism collapsing as man withdraws and looks inward. This fierce self-interest, which was brought about by a feeling that similar efforts on the part of nonwhite groups brought them benefits at the expense of the passive and apathetic white groups, will grow and become more powerful. It is ridiculous to deplore it. It is a fact of life of our times. Together with the general bitterness and dissatisfaction that plague all the groups that comprise the American majority, a mighty and, potentially dangerous force is rising. If there is no dialogue with them by the Jew, if the Jew does not forge close and regular links with these groups, he will find himself a minority challenged and threatened by this majority of minorities.

There is a great need for the Jew to gain the support or at least the active nonhostility of the huge American middle and the ethnic groups that comprise so much of it. They and not the American establishment, liberal or otherwise, are the wave of future, and the Jew must learn to swim in those waters and become familiar and confident in them.

Indeed, the creation of a Jewish power base to challenge the assaults on Jewish rights can get great impetus from an alliance with non-Jewish groups comprised, primarily, of lower- and low-middle-class individuals. The great danger to Jewish rights being an apathetic and fearful government, those politicians can be brought to deal by a coalition of Jews and other ethnic groups with the same problems.

Because of Jewish intellectualism, the Jew has tend-

ed to be cut off from these groups and this lack of com-
munications has reinforced much of their previous religious and socio-economic dislike of Jews. This gap must
be closed and the Jew must forge his ties with all the
groups he has ignored because they were not intellectual
enough, because they were not liberal enough, or because
we felt that they did not like Jews.

As to the massive stupidity on the part of many Jewish liberals to work with people who differ politically
and socio-economically, we have already spoken. We
should extend this principle of Jewish survival even to
working with people who may not like Jews. When concerned with Jewish survival one does not have to like
the person who can help him. If, for a momentary historical instance, the anti-Semite's interests coincide with
those of the Jew, let us learn to use that moment to our
own advantage. We have too many problems and too few
allies to be that fastidious—and stupid—over whose aid
we can afford to turn down.

Indeed, there is an immediate and concrete Jewish
need to have the aid of precisely this segment of the
American population. Their help is essential for the
struggle on behalf of the Soviet Jew.

WIN FREEDOM FOR SOVIET JEWS

If we hope to win freedom for enslaved Soviet Jewry,
we who were so late in bestirring ourselves, it is essential that we move swiftly and with a politically real,
imaginative, and bold program for their survival.

Let us not delude ourselves into believing that we

have the luxury of time in the battle for Soviet Jewry. Time is not, necessarily, on our side, and the possibility —or probability—of things taking a turn for the worse is high. The courageous and bold Jewish renaissance within the Soviet Union, with its Jews affirming their Jewishness, has shocked and angered a Kremlin that looks upon all this refusal to acknowledge the indivisibility of allegiance to the Soviet Union as treason. This, and a growing unrest by hawkish Politburo members in the face of general internal dissent, could very well lead to a neo-Stalinist crackdown on all dissent and Jewish dissent in particular. In the last years of Stalin's rule, climaxing with the fateful, final year of 1953, plans for a final solution of the Jewish problem in the USSR were drawn up. Hundreds of thousands of Jewish names were listed for deportation to Siberian camps, and it was only Stalin's death that saved Soviet Jewry. Let us not think that such a thing could not happen to a generation of Soviet Jews that has dared to "slander socialist Soviet reality."

Because of that, because of the proven failure of a past policy of silence, and because of the clear evidence that it was only the militant awakening of world Jewry in protests against the Soviet Jewish agony that opened, to an unprecedented degree, a crack in the Iron Curtain, it is essential that a new Soviet Jewry policy be adopted by us that will be built upon the following principles:

1. We must understand that action, bold and militant, audacious and imaginative, will and has helped Soviet Jews.

2. Freedom for Soviet Jewry begins by militantly taking their cause from the back pages of the newspapers and putting it—and keeping it—highlighted in the news media so as to make it a major concern of millions of people throughout the world who would otherwise rather not be bothered with it.

The Soviet Jewish problem cannot even begin to be resolved until people know about it in sufficient quantities and with sufficient indignation to make it an international cause célèbre. The world does not particularly wish to be bothered with causes, and particularly not Jewish ones. A cause becomes thrust upon people, and it requires long, laborious, and imaginative efforts to do so successfully.

Only when the Soviet Jewish question is taken off the middle pages and put on page one, à la Vietnam and other burning questions, will the first major step be taken towards its solution. Once this is done and a cause becomes "fashionable" and "glamorous" it enlists itself numerous youth who give of their time and sacrifices. It brings to itself the creativity of talented people and the zeal of numerous and diverse individuals anxious to motivate their lives with the excitement of a cause.

They will not, however, enlist in the cause unless they hear of it, unless it becomes a moral imperative. The news media are not prepared to make this a headline story unless there is in it the element of the dramatic, the sensational, the exciting.

It is because of this that the respectable, tepid undramatic rallies called by Establishment groups failed to arouse our news media. Like it or not, the attention of the world was finally focused on the problem by means of the violence unleashed by militant Jews, primarily of the Jewish Defense League. It was their "outrageous" actions which forced a world that would have rather slept to pay attention, that forced the Soviets to retreat in the face of world opinion, that gave incalculable moral support and spiritual strength to Soviet Jews, and that led moderate Jewish groups into unprecedented activity. Violence is not necessarily unthinking hooliganism; it can be a well thought out, responsible, political weapon. That lesson should not be forgotten; that kind of activity should be intensified and multiplied.

The fact that the Soviet Union is a massive power should not lead us to think that the battle is a hopeless one. The Soviets can be forced into concessions. The Soviets do not hold their prisoners out of unbending ideology. It is to their interest, at the moment, to let Jews go. If, on the other hand, by refusing them freedom the Russians can be made to believe that their interests will be harmed, they will reconsider.

Far more important to the Soviets than the Soviet Jewish question is their need for a detente with the West. Beset by the specter of Communist China, by a sluggish economy, by the financial squeeze caused by the need to satisfy growing consumer demands which feed political dissent, and the need to produce huge amounts of armaments for use in the West and on the Chinese border, the Kremlin is extremely anxious for a soothing of tensions with the United States and the NATO allies.

If this detente can be achieved and if bridges can be built to the West, a number of things might result that would aid the Soviet economy and allow them to concentrate on China and on domestic fence-building at home. Thus, disarmament and space talks can mean significant cuts in the hard-pressed Soviet budget. Given friendlier settings, trade talks and trade missions can be sponsored that would bolster the economy.

The Soviets have a huge stake in this détente, and it is the foundation of their foreign policy. This is why they attempt to improve their image with the Western public with cultural exchange programs and other international good-will missions. These serve as political tools for the Kremlin. They deaden the Western conscience. They anesthetize us and make us forget what they really are, for who can watch the Bolshoi and then walk out feeling quite as angry at the Soviets as before he walked in?

Knowing that the Soviets value this détente so highly and understanding its top-priority value to them, we must strike at the détente and was must threaten it. If the Soviets really feel that their image is being harmed and that their propaganda is being blunted, if they become fearful that détente may be threatened because of the Soviet Jewish issue, they will pause to reconsider.

The Soviets are an immensely pragmatic people. If the price for keeping Soviet Jews prisoners is too high— if the price is a possible loss of détente—they will not pay it. If on the other hand, they feel that obstacles to the détente can be cleared by paying the price of Soviet

Jewish freedom, they may bow to practicality.

Again the way to do this is to strike out in a bold, imaginative and couragous program. Militant and violent protest is an integral part of this; it brings to the attention of the world the Soviet Jewish plight and mars the image of the peaceful Russian. Thus, the disruption of Soviet concerts is not a mere act of hoodlumism but both a cry not to let Soviet culture deaden our consciences and an effort (that succeeds) in having the Soviets pull out these exchange programs.

On the other hand there are things that are non-violent that can also strike at the very heart of détente. I had hoped to present them to world leaders at Brussels so that they might throw their vast resources into action to implement them. But, man proposing and the Almighty disposing, it was not to be. Nevertheless, they are vital and they compose an imaginative and workable program of pressure against the détente that the Soviets value so:

a) An immediate suspension of all Western talks with the Soviet Union. This does *not* mean a break in diplomatic relations but only a temporary end to the trade, space, disarmament and other discussions which the Soviets want and need so very much.

b) An embargo on all trade with the Soviet Union and a general boycott of all firms doing business with the USSR.

c) An end to the cultural entertainment and sports exchanges which are used by the Soviets as political tools with which to deaden the world's conscience and gain sympathy from the Western public.

d) A campaign to discourage tourism to the Soviet Union except for the selected tourism specifically aimed at aiding oppressed peoples within the USSR.

e) A demand that the Soviet Union be barred from the Olympic Games and from other international organizations on the theory that she is no better than South Africa.

f) Legal harassment of Soviet officials, including picketing of private residences and mass telephone calls to diplomatic installations.

g) Nonviolent civil disobedience—for instance, sitdowns and chainings—to pressure world governments to suspend contacts with the USSR.

All of these aim at one thing: threatening to take away from the Soviets what they wish, today, most of all—détente. Soviet Jews are not worth the Kremlin's losing a major foreign policy objective. If the Jew can mount such a threat to that Soviet aim as to seriously threaten it, the Kremlin will quietly pay the price of Soviet Jewish freedom.

And then the third principle of a new Soviet Jewry policy is:

3. *We must understand that the key to making the Soviets move, lies not with Jews, but with non-Jews. In the West in particular, the President of the United States: That it is only by making the Soviet Jewish problem an American problem that the President will act.*

If we hope to make the Soviet Union move through

taking from them what they need and want most of all, it is not we who hold the key to this power. It is a non-Jewish key of which we speak here and it resides in the White House. As far as all the things that the Kremlin wants from the United States, it is Pennsylvania Avenue that giveth and taketh away.

It is the President's to declare or not to declare whether disarmament and trade talks will continue. It is his decision as to whether or not the process of building bridges will continue or be halted. His is the power —and his alone—to tell the Kremlin: No further meaningful progress can be made on the things that you desire unless some meaningful movement is seen on the Soviet Jewish problem.

Obviously, the President, following the fiasco of the Vietnam war and buffeted by a peace movement which urges and demands moves toward détente, is far less concerned with the Soviet Jewish problem than with the same bridges the Kremlin wants to build. The moral question of oppressed Soviet Jewry is forgotten in our delight at seeing bridges going up.

Because the President of the United States is not overly concerned with Jewish problems, we must take it out of that narrow and parochial Jewish realm and make it an international problem—most particularly, the problem of the President. This alone is what will cause him sufficient concern so as to move swiftly and emphatically.

How do we make this an international problem? Consider those actions that outrage the Russians so that relations between the two superpowers become strained. The harassment of Soviet diplomats is not an exercise in childishness as the more myopic would have us believe. There is no surer way to arouse the wrath of the Soviets than to have their officials humiliated and threatened.

It is this which takes the Soviet Jewish problem from a narrow, ethnic concern to one that forces the United States to take urgent action lest its main policy plank be threatened. At all costs the United States and the USSR are anxious to have their détente and this adds great leverage to our ability to pressure Washington into urging the Soviets—for the common interest of both super-powers—to make concessions on the Soviet Jewish issue.

Seeing so much pressure for an end to trade, disarmament, tourism, cultural and sports exchanges, watching violence against Soviet diplomats and fearing worse actions that could not only wreck all hope of détente but plunge the two nations into a crisis, the problem becomes a major one for the White House that could lead it to urge the Soviets to make concessions.

It is important, however, to make use of every conceivable pressure upon the President, and it is here that the non-Jewish American public is so important.

4. *We must learn to cultivate those individuals and groups nearest to the President regardless of who they are, and this approach must be done not on the basis of Jewish but of American or Western national interest.*

While it is true that at the final moment of crisis, the Jew should not expect help from others but must look to himself, nevertheless, in the short run and at a time when the problem is not acute, nor in its terminal stage, the Jew can and must look to non-Jewish help. The Soviet Jewish cause is an example of an issue which the Jew cannot solve alone and which calls for non-Jewish allies.

We must understand that in Middle America, conservative and anti-Communist, there is a vast number of non-Jewish Americans who are potential allies of the Soviet Jewish cause—and not because of any special love of Jews. Tens of millions of them understand quite well the nature of the Kremlin and realize that the Soviet Union's tyranny and aggression pose deadly threats to their own freedom and dignity. More, being religious people, they can understand the agony of Soviet Jews being religiously oppressed.

The approach to these potential allies must be made on a far more sophisticated basis than at present. The theme in the campaign to free Soviet Jews, as far as non-Jewish allies are concerned, must be one of enlightened American self-interest. The fate of Soviet Jews, it must be argued, is part of an entire approach to the Soviet Union, an approach that can either strengthen or jeopardize the freedom of the United States and the Free World. If the Soviets are allowed to freely oppress people without a restraining hand, if anti-Communism is allowed to become a pejorative thing, if accommodation to the Kremlin is allowed to override our concern for oppressed peoples, the Kremlin will surely become convinced of the decadence and weakness of the United States moral fiber and will grow ever bolder in its assaults on the Free World.

The President, it must be argued, came to power on a platform that promised a stronger and more vigorous opposition to Soviet oppression and imperialism. He must be held to his commitment and not allow Munich-type advisors to influence him to buy an illusory peace at the price of oppressed Soviet citizens.

It is not the liberal who will fight to pressure the President to get tough with Moscow. It is not the liberal who will call for the suspension of trade and talks with Moscow in order to free Russian Jewry. To the contrary, it is the liberal who is generally horrified at the slightest prospect of tensions between East and West. It is the liberal who will cry that the danger of war outweighs all other considerations. It is the liberal who, in all honest and decent belief, argues that détente and talks are the only ways to get freedom for the oppressed.

And the kind of people who are most understanding of the Soviet Jewish problem and who will be most sympathetic to our argument are precisely the members of the many ethnic groups who tend to make up conservative, anti-Communist Middle America. They are the ones with whom we must establish contacts and they are the ones we have most ignored.

This is true under any kind of administration but a thousand times more important under a President who is conservative and who needs these people in order to remain in office. As he needs their votes so must we desperately work to threaten to have those votes withheld because of his apathy and refusal to use meaningful pressure on behalf of Soviet Jewry.

This, at long last, is why it is so important to make meaningful contacts and ties with conservative groups. They can be organized into significant groups of Christians for Soviet Jewry that will be more meaningful politically to the White House than a thousand Jewish groups. The President needs them and we must move to have these groups demand a strong policy of pressure for Soviet Jewish freedom.

The Administration must be made to understand that not only Jewish voters but conservative anti-Communist voters will throw state after state to Democrats in a close election, *unless* he takes a strong stand on freedom for Soviet Jewry. Meetings with Presidential aides must be held; speaking tours must be arranged with churches, Rotaries, Kiwanis clubs, political clubs and other groups in the Administration's "Southern Strategy" states. As the drive against the Administration's refusal to pressure the Soviets on its Jews goes on; as committees consisting of Southern, Midwestern and Southwestern political leaders are being formed to demand an end to talks with the Soviets until they move on Soviet Jews; and as the White House Southern Strategy is imperiled, the full potential effects of this drive must be carefully explained to the White House and the solution carefully outlined:

The attack on the Administration's Southern Strategy will continue until the President uses his leverage with the Soviets to withhold from them what they want until they give in significantly on the Soviet Jewish issue.

This is a blueprint for liberation of Soviet Jewry that can prove to be effective. It breaks with fear and "respectability"; it demands innovation and imagination; it calls for courage and sacrifice; it breaks new ground. Above all, it gives an indication, for the first time, of possibilities for success in the battle for Soviet Jews, their rights, and freedom. The time to put it into practice is now, for tomorrow may be too late.

CHANGE THE IMAGE OF THE JEW

The Jew, with his persistent image of weakness, unwillingness and inability to fight back is open to constant physical attacks on the part of non-Jews. A youngster wearing a skull cap and returning from a yeshiva is fair game. Jews walking in a park or playing ball in a playground are open to attacks. Such things must be met in the one way that is most effective—a feeling on the part of the attacker that he stands an excellent chance of being severely beaten himself. Jews must be taught to defend themselves physically. This is the surest deterrent to attacks upon them.

Not only is the Jew who knows how to fight back hard and expertly saved from a beating, but his smashing of the hoodlum who attacked him will guarantee that the latter will think much more carefully about attacking a Jew the next time. But, more important, is the cumulative effect of a large number of Jews fighting back and pummeling their attackers—the changing of the image of the Jew.

There is no surer guarantee that the Jew will be the subject of attacks than the feeling that Jews do not fight back or cannot fight back. The implementing of a major, well-publicized program of Jewish strength-building and a professional program of self-defense training (karate, street fighting, etc.) will go a long way toward burying that image.

Every Jewish Day School and synagogue must begin such a program without falling victim to the tired and nonsensical cliché that such things will create tension. No anti-Semite has ever been created because Jews fight back. Jewish strength, Barzel, is indeed a Jewish concept. It always has been and always will be so long as we live in a world where the Jew is an object of attack. Those Jews who differ with this concept are, generally, those who are not under attack. By their persistence in opposing Jewish self-defense, they perpetuate the image of the Jewish lemming. They gain nothing but non-Jewish contempt and guarantee further attacks upon Jews—all Jews, including themselves.

The mass program of Jewish physical defense must include not only strengthening bodies and learning the various means of self-defense, but also a well-financed and professionally supervised program of proficiency in firearms with every Jew having a legal weapon in his home.

Why? To ask that question of a people which lost so many of its number a short while ago because it failed to acquire or learn how to use firearms; to ask that question of Jews who live in neighborhoods that are cesspools of crime and violence; to ask that of us who are threatened by a myriad of groups with all manner of horrors; to ask that of Jews who know that every other group does not hesitate to buy and know how to use firearms—is difficult to understand. We cannot repeat ourselves too often. We pray that we may never have to use such weapons. Should we have to, however, it is better to know how. Indeed, this well-publicized Jewish program will help to bury that past image of the Jew as one easily feasted upon. A Jewish home with a firearm is a safer home. A Jewish neighborhood filled with weapons and people who know how to use them will give the hooligan pause. Jewish rifle clubs, sponsored by the proper rifle associations, should be organized and Jewish schools should enroll their students in them. We know that we will not use the weapcns in anger or in offense. Are we so sure that others will exercise the same caution against us?

SAFEGUARD JEWISH RIGHTS

We have spoken earlier of such threats to Jewish rights as crime, poverty, changing neighborhoods, and reverse discrimination. All of these must be met with a concerted program of Jewish Power.

On Crime and Violence

The problem of crime must be met with powerful community pressure on the police to do their job. In too many cases, the police are either unable or unwilling to act. Should the answer continue to be the inevitable, "We do not have enough men," our rejoinder must be that *we* do. We cannot sit back and allow police impotency to doom Jewish neighborhoods to a future of crime and violence and eventual oblivion as panic-stricken people move out.

Hopefully, the threat to take matters into our own hands will serve as a gadfly to prod the police into doing their function. If the police, however, still fail to do their job, self-defense patrols should be set up, made up of individuals, both on foot and in automobiles, carrying two-way radios, and legally armed—those licensed to carry firearms should do so, others should carry appropriate objects which are legal and also effective. We are committed to law in a democracy, but that law must be a two-way street, and the police must enforce the law for *everybody*.

As for the absurd cry of "vigilantes," it is clear that a vigilante group is one which, despite the fact that there is adequate law enforcement, takes the law into its own hands and executes summary justice. When we have seen, over weeks and months and years that, for whatever reason given, the police have proven themselves inadequate to enforce the basic duties of a state, it is criminal *not* to act. Since the state's basic function is the protection of life, liberty and property, when that state fails its responsibilities because of lack of sufficient police or indifference or whatever, the innocent victims of crime and violence must be protected.

These patrols whose function is to cover both buildings and streets should be furnished copies of the pertinent paragraphs in the criminal code relating to the citizen's right to apprehend criminals. When a crime is seen being committed, the police should be informed by radio and the crime stopped by the patrol. If captured, the criminal should be held for the police. Well-publicized notices of the formation of these patrols should be made in adjoining non-Jewish neighborhoods where most of the criminals usually come from.

Every synagogue which has been vandalized or which is in a crime-ridden neighborhood should be equipped with an alarm system that attaches both to the local police precinct and the local patrol headquarters. If the synagogue cannot afford this, the money for it must come from the community.

Merchants must be protected from the bolder robbers who prey upon them. A well-publicized campaign of armed guards in selected stores (the exact ones are, naturally, not disclosed) will go a long way to safeguarding these stores.

Schools must be made safe for the teachers and students who attend them. Principals must be made to understand that they are expected to see to the safety of their schools and to move swiftly against those students they know are guilty of attacks upon others. Failure to do so should be followed by leaflets at the schools announcing that hoodlums who attack will be dealt with in the proper manner and asking youngsters and teachers who have been assaulted to step forward and give details. Such a program will invariably find the authorities awakening with a new-found zeal to do what they should have been doing all along.

In order to save neighborhoods that are afflicted with crime from an exodus of Jews that would doom the area, attacks on crime must be joined with an assault on the "block-buster," that real estate individual who uses tactics of fear and panic to force people to move and sell their homes. Lists of such block-busters should be gathered and each one visited with boycotts, picket signs and uninhibited warnings to cease and desist. At the same time, nonprofit commercial real estate listings should be set up which will insure that Jewish areas will be preserved.

There are, of course, destroyed neighborhoods— once-Jewish neighborhoods—that are beyond hope, where almost all the Jews have left and, yet, where a remnant of elderly, poverty-stricken Jews remain, caught in a nightmare of crime and terror. Careful censuses of these areas should be taken and the elderly moved out by Jewish organizations, with our federations subsidizing these poor people in the more expensive apartments of new neighborhoods.

Poverty

The problem of poverty must be dealt with in all its aspects. The most powerful pressure imaginable must be brought to bear on government to make sure that Jews get their proper share of anti-poverty funds and their proper representation on poverty councils. This protest should take the form of demonstrations, law suits, and sit-ins. Similar action should be taken to insure that any deserving Jew gets government loans for small business.

Strong pressure must also be brought against local Jewish federations with demands that they reorder their priorities to allocate funds for educational scholarships and rent subsidies for the Jewish poor.

A regular battery of lawyers must be on retainer and on call to file law suits for poor Jewish defendants and against government and nongoverment offices that refuse to recognize their rights.

Nonprofit community employment bureaus should be set up, as well, to insure that employment opportunities will be made known to applicants swiftly and without bias or discrimination. Similar community loan centers should be established.

Reverse Discrimination

Once again, law suits, demonstrations, and sit-ins must be used to safeguard the rights of Jews who are victims of discrimination—either of the traditional or reverse kind. Offices must be set up where data will be gathered for deserving students turned down by schools (schools whose college-entrance policies admit non-Jews while Jews must face competitive examinations), teachers dismissed, civil servants denied promotion.

All these above problems, however, are so complex and pervasive that only a mass joining-together of Jews into neighborhood organizations that exercise great political, economic, and social power can solve them.

Such a group should understand that government is movable only by groups that protest the loudest and that exercise the kind of power that threatens the politician with fall from power. This is why Jewish Power is so important.

If Jewish neighborhoods organize into federated councils, with this body implementing the above program of safeguarding Jewish rights by the use of funds gathered from every synagogue and by voluntary taxes paid by residents and merchants in the area, powerful and potent Jewish Power groups are established. If, in addition, these groups serve as political guides to Jewish residents, advising them how to vote and for whom to vote based strictly on Jewish interests, their power becomes immense. Jewish Power—this is the answer to the safeguarding of Jewish rights and the survival of the Jew at a time that government is capitulating to other groups and acquiescing in the erosion and destruction of Jewish rights.

Any program for Jewish survival must be built upon all of these foundations: Jewish pride and identity, a gathering together of Jewish resources to fight first and foremost for Jewish causes and to solve Jewish problems, the building of a Jewish political, social and, economic power structure, a determination to do this and whatever else is necessary on behalf of the Jewish people.

CONCLUSION

This is an outrageous book and much of what is written in it will disturb and infuriate many people. No matter. Men whose lives are carefully built about satisfying other people and who fear to speak out lest they go against the prevailing winds are hardly men, while those who insist on others agreeing with them are hardly worth concerning ourselves about.

Our problems are that we live lives of quiet fears. We are afraid of countless things that are mostly non-existent or unimportant. What we are most afraid of is being in a minority. We tend to assume that because a majority believes a certain way it must be correct. When that majority is composed of wealthy and prestigious people and organizations, we are convinced of it. Power intimidates us and powerful people, with supreme contempt for commoners, know this and utilize it.

But majorities are not always right, and the fact that the sane running of a democratic society calls for the minority to accept the mandate of the majority, still does not mean that the mandate is blessed with truth. Indeed, when it comes to the question of principles and ideals there is a rebuttable presumption that the ruling powers are correct. Those who hold the seat of power seek to cleave to that power and are motivated, not so much by truth, but by self-interest. This is not the surest guarantee of attaining truth.

Let us never fear being a minority. We are the minority *par example* and have survived it with honor. Let us not be terrified or intimidated by the thought of being alone, the one person in the crowd who disagrees, the one who is convinced of the truth of his position and who cries out his opposition. Let us not back down before the fury and storm of prestige and power. It is not easy to stand alone against the crowd or the power brokers. It means derision, threats, defamation, and loneliness. It is so much easier to drift with the tide rather than swim against it. Man is happier that way; he has fewer problems.

That is not the way of a man; that is certainly not the way of a Jew. If the Jew had accepted the premise that the majority must be right, he would long since have disappeared from the stage of history. If he had capitulated before the power and prestige of kings and churchmen, he would have long ceased being a Jew. If he had been intimidated by numbers and reputation he would not have been the son of Abraham that he is.

They called our father, Avraham HaIvri—Abraham, the Hebrew. And the word Ivri, Hebrew, comes from the word "eyver" or "side." The whole world stood on one side and Abraham on the other. The whole world said that theirs was the way and Abraham dissented. In the end, he was right and all the others wrong. In the end he was proven right only because he had the courage to endure the loneliness of the long distance rebel. We are his children.

To dissent is not easy and to be a rebel is more than difficult, but no great revolution has ever taken place in Jewish history that was not begun and concluded by rebels willing to risk that loneliness and the storm of hatred and attack that was leveled at them.

" 'Everybody is wrong, you alone are right?' No doubt this question springs by itself to the readers lips and mind. It is customary to answer this with apologetic phrases to the effect that I fully respect public opinion, that I bow to it, that I was glad to make concessions. . . . All that is unnecessary and untrue. You cannot believe in anything in this world if you admit even once that perhaps your opponents are right, and not you. This is not the way to do things. There is but one truth in the world and it is all yours. If you are not sure of it stay at home; but if you are sure, don't look back and it will be your way. . . ."

These are the words of Zev Jabotinsky, the supreme Jewish rebel of our time. Only because of such words and such a stubborn Jew did all the outrageous concepts he advanced and all the rebellious ideas that he propagated finally come into being. There is a Jewish State today because Theodor Herzl, when refused a permit to hold the Zionist Congress in Munich because of Jewish Establishment pressure on the authorities, refused to abandon the idea, he held it in Basle instead. He was a rebel. There is a State of Israel today because the Jewish underground, Irgun and Sternists, were attacked and assaulted by Jewish leaders, but they insisted to the end they were right. They were rebels.

"You alone are right?" If you believe so, shout it forth: "Yes, I am right and I will fight for the day when you, too, understand." Such a man must be prepared to look at the angry, hate-filled faces of his opponents, those who cannot forgive his defiance and courage. He must look at them and choose greatness together with loneliness, enmity and opposition!

It is not important.

He must have within him the iron and steel to move forward against obstacles that will be placed in his path at all times; to move against the fierce storm of opposition; to fly in the face of personal attacks and insults; to stand up to the slings and arrows of his opponents and the protests of even those he loves. Little men cannot abide giants in spirit; they remind them of their own weaknesses. They envy and resent those who carry within them the gift of vision; they must be destroyed. No matter.

He must have within him the unbending strength to move forward resolutely in spite of those attacks. He must have within him a sense of values and must understand that which is truly important—not by bread alone shall man live. He will be discouraged. He will be depressed by failures. He must learn that patience that comes from iron. He must have the confidence that comes from the steel within him.

Why? Because he loves Jews and because Jews need him and because someone must do what has to be done. Because he cares about his brother and loves his sister and is moved by some compelling force to help even while being condemned.

Because in his mind he has seen the mounds of corpses and visited the camps where they killed us. Because he stands in the now empty rooms where once Jews were driven to stand in their nakedness and breathe their last. Because while he stands alone he does not stand alone. Because, by his side, are the ghosts of those who are no longer, whose blood was shed like water because Jewish blood was considered cheap. Because he has seen their outstretched hands and looked into the burning and soul-searing eyes of tragedy that peered into his very being and heard them say:

"Never again. Promise us, *never again.*"